First edition for North America published in 2005 by
Barron's Educational Series, Inc.

Copyright © **MQ Publications Limited 2005**
Text copyright © **Ian Keable 2005**
Editor: **Karen Ball**
Design: **Balley Design Associates**
Photography: **Steve Tanner**

All inquiries should be addressed to:
Barron's Educational Series, Inc.
250 Wireless Boulevard
Hauppauge, New York 11788
www.barronseduc.com

ISBN-13: 978-0-7641-3222-3
ISBN-10: 0-7641-3222-9

Library of Congress Catalog Card No. 2005922473

Printed and bound in China

9 8 7 6 5 4 3 2 1

the big book of MAGIC fun

Ian Keable

BARRON'S

cOntents

6   About the Author

7   Foreword

8   The Props You Will Need

10   The Story of Magic

12   Close-up Magic

17   Comedy Magic

24   Big Magic

34   Silent magic

44   Mind Magic

51   Dangerous Magic

60   The Secrets of Tricks

62   Floating Ruler

64   Magic Compass

66   Flying Cards

70   Bluff Book Test

72   Thumb Fun

74   Cut and Restored String

77   Levitating Tumbler

78   Through the Glass

80   Boxes and Balls

84   Matching Cards

86   Friendly Trick

89   Time Please

90   Rising Matchbox

92   Loop the Loop

94   Coin in Glass

96   Quick Escape

98   Torn and Restored Napkin

101   Paddling Knife

102   Knife and Paper

104   Taking a Bow

106   Number Confusion

108   Banana Split

110   Bangle and Ribbon

112 Quick Release
114 Coins Across
118 Jumping Toothpick
119 Slot-Machine Hand
122 Notable Number
124 Not a Knot
126 X-Ray Crayons
128 Bank Roller
130 Card Prediction
132 Solid through Solid
134 Straw Cutting
138 Balloon Burst
140 Bow and Arrow
142 Frustrating Pencil
144 Disappearing Coin
146 Glass through Table
150 Endless Chain

154 Sleight of Hand

158 How to Control a Card
159 The Overhand Shuffle
162 Selection of the Card
164 Return of the Card
165 Control of the Card
168 How to Force a Card
170 Tracker Card
174 Jumping Card
176 Name Spelling
178 How to Conceal a Coin
182 Make a Coin Disappear
184 Make a Coin Appear
186 Change One Coin for Another
188 Copper Silver Coin Trick

190 Index

192 Picture Credits

About the Author

Ian Keable has been a full time magician since 1990. His specialty is stand-up comedy magic. He is a Member of The Inner Magic Circle (the most prestigious magic society in the UK) and also the British Ring of the International Brotherhood of Magicians. He has won the British Championship of Comedy Magic. He has performed magic not only on television but also on the radio!

With many thanks to our models Elizabeth Maskell and Hugo Hadlow who are both members of the Young Magicians Club, part of The Magic Circle's youth initiative.

Foreword

Magic is as popular today as it ever was. Despite the attraction of computer games and state-of-the-art movies, nothing is more impressive than seeing the amazing happen live. Everybody likes magic because it taps into our love of wonder and the unknown. *The Big Book of Magic Fun* will make you part of that world by teaching you some fun magic.

Most of the book consists of tricks. You are not expected to learn them all! Just look through them and find one or two that appeal to you for whatever reason. Maybe it is the particular prop it uses; maybe it is the impact you expect it to have on your audience; maybe the way of doing it seems intriguing. Some tricks may appear very difficult at first. But you can always come back to them later on when you have mastered some easier ones.

When you read how some of the tricks work, you may be surprised how simple they are. You might think nobody will be taken in. But spectators always imagine tricks are much harder than they actually are. They look for the complicated solution and miss the obvious one.

That is one reason why you should never reveal your secrets. Your audience will feel very let down if they discover how easily they were fooled. And you will lose all the credit for being clever. It is worth repeating: never reveal your secrets.

Many tricks done by professional magicians are simple ones. Indeed they perform many of those explained in this book. What makes them stand out in the hands of an expert is that they work hard on all the other features that turn a trick into magic. Magicians call this "presentation."

You will find plenty of advice on different aspects of presentation in the non-trick sections of the book. So even if you are not interested in doing Mind Magic or Silent Magic, they are still worth reading. You will also learn about some of the best known magicians and the history of magic; which can only help in making you a better magician.

For example some beginners think their hands are too small; and use that as an excuse not to practice. However, one of the best magicians in the eighteenth century was Matthew Buchinger. He was only 29 inches tall and had tiny arms. He became a master of conjuring dexterity.

Most of the book is best read by dipping in and out of it. This is not the case with the Sleight of Hand section. Here it is advisable to go through the various sleights in the order they are written. Even though you do not need to be able to do any of these sleights to perform the other tricks in the book, they help greatly in general handling skills.

Above all, though, the aim of this book is to show you why magic is so much fun. The tricks are fun to do: they are certainly fun to watch; and they should even be fun to practice. If you have fun with your magic, then everybody around you will have fun too. Welcome to *The Big Book of Magic Fun*.

Ian Keable, 2005

The Props You Will Need

The apparatus which magicians do their magic with are called props. The props in this book are everyday items that can be found around the home or are easily obtained.

Cards and Coins

It's likely you already have a deck of playing cards in the home, just waiting for that rainy day or long journey. Sometimes it is better to use a deck that has been broken in, which means the cards are softened and therefore easier to handle. Professional magicians often prefer to work with slightly larger cards than most people normally use, and these can be bought from magic shops or websites.

You'll want to find a few coins to add to your burgeoning collection of props. Larger coins are easier for the magician to handle and the audience to see. Foreign coins can bring an extra touch of the exotic to your show. You can ask parents if they have any coins left over from trips abroad or ask at a foreign currency exchange or a bank.

Unlikely Props

You wouldn't expect paper cups and wax crayons (right) to necessarily be part of a magic show, but these are just the types of carefully chosen props that this book uses. We don't ask you to spend a lot of money or track down obscure suppliers. You should be able to start your magic right away!

An Element of Creativity

Some of the tricks ask you to make your props in advance. You might need to do a certain amount of measuring, cutting out, and coloring in as with the props for Magic Compass. In fact, this process allows you to really think about what it is you need from your props and what you are trying to achieve with the trick. Is it better that the magic compass is the same color card on both sides, or do you prefer to have two different color sides? Which makes the trick work best? Exactly how long should the string be for Cut And Restored String? As you experiment, you will see how crucial every detail is to the success of a trick.

Planning Ahead

Tricks such as Straw Cutting require you to adapt your props before you begin performing—in this case, by cutting a slit in the straw. This means that not all is as it seems as you begin a trick. You know this, but the audience doesn't. A magician is only as good as his or her props and to this end, you always need to make sure that all your props are prepared by you and no one else.

Above and left ➤ Most of the props you will need for magic tricks can easily be found around the home, such as crayons, handkerchiefs, toothpicks, string, coins, scissors, and drinking straws.

Close-up Magic

Close-up magic is performed very near to your spectators, usually for only a small group. The size of the prop can determine whether it is close up—for instance, a trick with rubber bands is hard to see from far away. More often though it is a question of whether the audience needs to be close in order to fully understand the plot.

Close-up magic has many advantages over other types of magic—it can be performed almost anywhere and at any time; you need only one or two individuals to create a show and people are more appreciative when the magic is happening right in front of their eyes. For these reasons it is probably the best magic to concentrate on when you first start performing magic.

Learning Close-up Magic

Most of the tricks in this book are suitable for close-up magic. Read through them and find one that appeals to you. You then need to practice it. The Sleight of Hand section (page 154) gives some tips on this.

When you feel comfortable with what you have to do and say, you must find an audience. The best way to learn how to be a magician is by doing it; you will soon discover the more you perform, the better you will become. So sometimes it can be better to throw yourself in the deep end, and find some willing spectators, rather than practicing on your own too much. Close-up magic gives you many opportunities to show your tricks; whether you are at school, with friends at home, or at a party, you can do some magic.

The hardest part of magic when you begin is the worry that you might be found out. This is bound to happen occasionally and can be embarrassing,

although remember, it is probably of more concern to you than to your audience. Treat it as a learning experience. Work out why the secret was discovered, practice some more, and make the necessary corrections so it does not happen again. The better magicians tend to perform the same tricks for different people, rather than different tricks for the same people. It is therefore best to really concentrate on learning one or two tricks well. There is the story of a young boy speaking to the famous magician David Devant. He said, "I know 49 tricks—how many do you know?" Devant said he knew eight! However, Devant knew everything about the tricks inside out, as he had done them hundreds of times.

As part of learning your tricks you also need to learn how to make them convincing for your audience. An important part of this is called "misdirection."

Misdirection

In all magic, misdirection is important, however it is best understood in the context of close-up magic. There are two golden rules that are vital to learn:

• If you want your audience to look at something, you look at it too. This works because it is natural for people to follow your eyes; they assume what you are looking at is important, so they want to look at it too.

• If you want your audience to look away from something, look at them. If you look directly at them, they assume that you want to communicate something and will return your gaze.

Here is an example where you can make use of this. Imagine you are about to do The French Drop as taught in the Sleight of Hand section (page 154).

Hold the coin in your hand and look at it. Your spectators will look at it too. Start to move your other hand toward the coin and, as you do so, look at your audience. They will meet your eye. This means that when you actually perform The French Drop, nobody should be looking directly at your hands. As your hand moves away, supposedly holding the coin, look toward it. Again your audience will follow your gaze. They should lose interest in the other hand, which has the coin in it.

Even if you perform The French Drop very well, misdirection is still important. This is because you want to make it hard for anyone to recall the chain of events that took place. Through your misdirection you have taken attention away from the disappearance, so when people try to recreate what happened, the chances are they will have forgotten you did the move at all. Their chances of figuring out exactly how the trick is done are therefore minimal.

Right ➤ Magician David Blaine amazes his audience with his daring tricks.

Close-up Magicians

The King of Close-up Magic

If you find you are having problems mastering a particular trick, then try to improve it by making subtle alterations. You might want to take your inspiration from the brilliant Dai Vernon.

Most magicians would agree that Vernon was the most influential close-up magician in the history of magic. Dai Vernon was born in Canada but lived most of his life in the United States. Although he was an excellent performer, he was best known for developing new sleights and routining. Routining means taking an existing trick and making it more entertaining by altering the structure and presentation. It is a similar procedure that a musician might go through in coming up with a new arrangement for a piece of music.

Many of his best routines are written up in *The Dai Vernon Book of Magic*, which was published in 1957. Perhaps his most famous is the Cups and Balls. The trick itself dates back over 2,000 years. In most variations, small balls jump around between three cups. At the finish the cups are tipped over to reveal three completely different objects. These loads, as they are called, could be large balls, fruit, or even small chickens. Vernon came up with a routine that not only seamlessly blended many innovative sleights but provided natural misdirection for secretly placing the loads under the cups.

Dai Vernon died in 1992 at the age of 99. He was an enthusiastic teacher and mentor right to the end. He was known simply as "The Professor."

The Elmsley Count

Next time you see a magician count out four cards, make sure you look very carefully. Alex Elmsley invented a method for counting where one card is counted twice, cleverly hiding another in the process. It is known as the Elmsley Count.

Alex Elmsley has never been a full-time magician. When he was young there was little opportunity to earn a living in the United Kingdom from close-up magic. Instead, he joined the ranks of the many amateurs responsible for inventing tricks used by professionals. His prolific output is consolidated in two books of 400 pages each. Given that for the vast majority of his working life Elmsley took no interest in magic at all, devoting himself to his career in computers—it is an awe-inspiring body of work.

He is perhaps fortunate in having a sleight named after him. Most inventors are not so lucky and they fail to obtain the recognition they so richly deserve. This is the reason why nobody knows who invented so many great tricks in magic.

Today's Kings of Close-up

It's impossible to choose a single current king of close-up. There is Juan Tamariz from Spain, who combines technical brilliance with a zany personality; Lennart Green from Sweden, who has turned card magic on its head with completely original sleights; Ricky Jay from the United States, who brings a love of magic history and sublime patter to his presentations; and David Williamson, also from the United States, who is constantly improvising during his funny and superbly executed routines.

A close-up magician who does stand out is René Lavand from Argentina. One of his best tricks is called Oil and Water, in which black and red cards are mixed together but they magically separate. He repeats this trick over and over using the running catchphrase: "I can't do it any slower." He can also false shuffle and cut a deck of cards.

Admittedly, there are other magicians who display similar skills. The difference is that René Lavand has only one arm!

Magic for Magicians

Magicians don't just perform in front of Joe Public. They also like to entertain themselves! Some magicians enjoy showing tricks and fooling each other; and when they do, it is mostly with close-up magic. Magicians talk about "underground" magic, magic that only a select few know about. These magicians joke they are members of the Secret Seven which is so secret they don't even know who the other six members are!

There are some magicians who earn a good living performing mainly for other magicians. This is done principally at lectures and magic conventions. At lectures they explain how their tricks are done. At a convention they might perform in a show without giving explanations. Magic is a universal language and at conventions there are magicians from all over the world performing for each other.

Another opportunity for magicians to meet and swap tricks with each other is at magic clubs. There are magic clubs in every country and in most major cities all over the world. The best-known magic club in the United Kingdom is The Magic Circle, based in London. In the United States there is The Magic Castle in Los Angeles. The latter is a dining club that is open to the general public to see magic.

Cheating at Cards

Magicians perform tricks and learn their sleights for fun. They do not use their skills to cheat at cards. However, many magicians are fascinated by some of the sleights that card cheats might employ and can often perform them much better than the card cheats themselves.

The interest in cheating techniques mainly arises from a book written by S.W. Erdnase in 1902 called *The Expert at the Card Table*. Erdnase was a professional gambler but beyond that, nobody knows anything about him. In his book he went into detail about all the methods of the professional card cheat and showed how many of them could be adapted and used by magicians purely for the sake of entertainment.

The hardest card-cheating sleight is considered to be false dealing. Second dealing is where you deal the second card in the deck instead of the top card and bottom dealing is where you deal the bottom card instead of the top. The most difficult of all is center dealing, where it looks like you are dealing the top card of the deck but you are actually taking it from the center. Only a handful of magicians in the world can do this well.

Location! Location! Location!

Working a Room

If you're going to get paid for your magic, you need to know how to work a room. In other words, do your magic right under people's noses while also keeping them entertained.

Close-up magicians can be booked to perform in restaurants, at banqueting halls, and at party receptions. The magician normally has a number of tricks that are repeated as he or she goes around the room. Most keep all their props in their pockets or in a small bag they carry around with them. The best tricks to do are those that are instantly resettable. This means that no special preparation needs to be done in advance before performing the trick in question.

One of the earliest professional close-up magicians was Bert Allerton. He used to perform in a very trendy restaurant in Chicago in the 1940s. If you requested it, he would come over and sit down at your table to do magic for you. Besides being an excellent performer, he was also very charming and had a great sense of humor. Charm and humor: two of the essential ingredients for good magic.

Close-up Magic on the Small Screen

No detail is too miniscule to be picked up by a television camera. For this reason, close-up magic works particularly well as a camera can pick out the smallest prop. One of the earliest pioneers was Don Alan who had his own series on ABC television called "The Magic Ranch" in 1962. Other magicians such as the illusionist Doug Henning, the brilliant all around Dutchman Fred Kaps, and David Nixon from the United Kingdom also successfully performed close-up magic on television as part of their magic shows.

Recently, the whole presentation of close-up magic on television has been revolutionized by the performer David Blaine. Rather than filming in a television studio in front of an invited audience, Blaine performs to strangers in the street. Their response to the magic appears to be much less contrived. Blaine understood that the reaction of the audience is just as important as the tricks; the camera focuses on those watching the magic as much as it does on the performer.

Magic Takes to the Stage

There are some magicians who perform tricks that are normally considered to be close-up, but on stage in a theater. One such magician was Nate Leipzig, who was born in Sweden, but emigrated to the United States as a child. He used to perform a trick called the Color Change—by passing your hand in front of a deck of cards, the face card changes to a different one. There is no way that most people could see the change. But the reaction of enjoyment and amazement of those up on stage with him conveyed it to the rest of the audience.

By all accounts, Nate Leipzig was a true gentleman. He once sat with a friend watching somebody perform his exact same act, the worst insult someone can inflict on a fellow performer. His companion pointed out, "Nate, he's stolen your act." Leipzig nodded in agreement, "But he's doing it so well."

Comedy Magic

A lot of magic is funny; audiences often laugh when they are surprised. So whatever type of magic you do, the chances are you will cause amusement from time to time. However, with comedy magic performers deliberately try to get as many laughs as they can. This can be achieved either by what they say, which magicians call "patter," or what they do.

So, How Do You Get the Laughs?

Comedy Patter

The most common way to get laughs is to say something funny. When magicians do this they call them "lines." For instance, you tell someone to shuffle the deck but keep the cards in the same order. Or you pick up a green silk handkerchief and say, "I have here a white handkerchief which is green." You might be performing a trick where you claim to have made a coin disappear from your hand. You say, "That was the easy part; the difficult bit is making it come back again."

Some magicians like to use puns, which are plays on words. Remove a felt pen from your pocket and say, "I know it's a felt pen because I felt it." Cut a piece of rope and remark that it is frightened, "Look, the end is frayed (afraid)." Puns work particularly well with children; but if there are too many of them, adults can find them less amusing.

The best patter suits your own personality or character. Just because a line works for one person does not mean it works as well for someone else. You tell someone, "Show the playing card to your friends—that shouldn't take long." Most people would find that rather rude; it would be funny only if it suits your delivery style. Try your lines out on close family and friends—they'll soon let you know if they are not funny!

It is important when practicing a trick to think about what you are going to say as much as what you are going to do. Always be on the lookout for funny lines; sometimes in performance either you or a spectator may say something unexpected that gets a laugh. If this happens, write it down and use it again.

Situation Comedy

Rather than saying something funny, it is possible to get laughs by creating amusing situations. For example, audiences like it when tricks appear to have gone wrong, so borrowing somebody's money and apparently burning it is a very popular trick. Another one is pretending you have smashed somebody's watch.

Comedy is often much easier to perform when you have someone from out of your audience to assist you. If this person seems to make a mistake, that can be funny. You ask somebody to hold onto the deck of cards, and when you are not looking they shuffle them.

You can also get your assistant to do something silly that will make everybody else laugh. You could get a boy to wear a pink paper hat or give a girl a magic wand that collapses when she holds it. Magicians call this type of situation "bits of business." You will find that the funniest magicians have plenty of bits of business.

Try and work out why audiences laugh at certain things you do. Be on the lookout for bits of business that make people laugh. A good comedy magician can make the most serious trick amusing.

Looking Funny

Although not all comedy magicians look funny, it can certainly help: an audience relaxes and laughs before the magician has even said a word. Carlton was a British magician who was long and thin; he made himself look even taller by wearing a bald wig. He also spoke in a high-pitched voice. He used to make jokes about the fact that he was so thin: "I haven't disappeared—I've only turned sideways. People think they know how my tricks are done because they can see the wires. They are not wires; they are my legs."

Al Flosso was an American magician who spoke in a voice rather like the well-known juggler W.C. Fields. He was short and squat. He would say to a young boy, "Are you married?" The boy would reply, "No." Flosso would advise, "Stay that way—look at me, I'm all shrunk up."

You can still be funny, however, if you look normal. In some ways this can work better because the humor is more unexpected.

Comedy Gags

There are plenty of gags that are not really magic, but are fun to do between proper magic tricks. It's important not to forget that most people enjoy a good laugh just as much as they enjoy seeing good magic. Here are some amusing bits of business you can try.

Place a handkerchief over your left hand. Your right hand holds the center of the handkerchief and lifts it up and down as if something is about to appear. Whip the handkerchief off and reveal your finger sticking up.

Tell someone to take any coin out of their pocket and to keep it hidden from you. Say you will tell them what the date is. They think you are going to say the date on the coin, but you just announce today's date.

Prepare a newspaper by cutting out a hole in one of the inside pages, large enough to fit your head through. Turn the outer pages upside down. Pretend to read the newspaper. People will start looking at you as the paper is apparently upside down. When you have everybody's attention, turn the page over and stick your head out of the hole.

Hold a paper bag in one hand between your finger and thumb. With the other hand throw an imaginary coin in the air. Pretend to catch it in the bag. At the same time flick your finger and thumb. The bag makes a snapping noise and moves, just as if the coin had landed inside it.

Although simple, they can get a better reaction than many tricks.

Right ➤ Tommy Cooper, a master of cod magic. See page 20 for Cod Magic.

Putting the Laughs into Magic

Funny Tricks

All tricks can be funny, if presented in a particular way. However there are some tricks that have humor built into them. One such trick is The Banana-Bandana trick. A bandana is a colored handkerchief. The magician is listening to some instructions on a tape that tell him how to make a bandana disappear. Unfortunately, he confuses a bandana for a banana. So when he or she is told to fold the bandana in half, the banana gets squashed and squelched everywhere.

Another example of a funny trick is when rolled-up paper balls disappear right in front of someone's face. It is amusing because the rest of the audience can see where they go, but the helper has no idea. This trick was made famous by an Italian-born magician named Slydini. Both David Copperfield in the United States and Paul Daniels in the United Kingdom have performed different versions of this trick, so it has stood the test of time.

Cod Magic

When you're looking for laughs, you don't even have to perform real magic. Cod magic is a parody of a magical performance involving the deliberate exposure of a simple magic effect for laughs. An audience enjoys being in on the joke. The best-known U.S. cod magician is Carl Ballantine. When he shows how a trick works, his catch phrase is: "How else?" The most famous cod magician in the U.K. was Tommy Cooper, who deliberately got his tricks wrong. He was so funny that people thought of him more as a comedian than a magician.

Being a bad magician on purpose can be amusing, but just being bad through lack of practice is not. The best cod magicians are just as skilled as the suave and sophisticated magicians.

An example of cod magic is to take a well-known trick, then put in an amusing twist. Swedish magician, Johnny Lonn, places a large radio under a cloth. Everybody expects that when he throws the cloth up in the air the radio will disappear, but instead it crashes to the floor.

The Location of Comedy

Comedy Clubs

A place to learn how to be funny is in comedy clubs. These mostly feature stand-up comedians; but magicians can work in these as well, providing they get plenty of laughs. Mac King is one of the funniest magicians in the world today and now has his own show in Las Vegas. He learned his trade in comedy clubs. Mac admits he got very few laughs when he started out. It was only through constant performing that he found a style that suited him.

In his show Mac performs tricks such as making his head disappear in a bag and appearing to eat a live goldfish. He also pretends he is invisible by putting on a cloak of invisibility and walking around the stage on tip toe.

Comedy Magic and Television

There are not many magicians who have become famous on television through comedy magic. A man who did is Paul Daniels, who had his own magic series on BBC television for more than ten years. One of his most hilarious pieces involved doing magic with some chimpanzees. They seemed to be intrigued by something hidden inside a box, even though the box was to all appearances empty. It turned out the bottom of the box was in fact a mirror, and the chimps were simply staring at their own reflection.

Paul Daniels learned his magic in clubs and cabaret venues all over the United Kingdom. His audiences could be very difficult and he would often get heckled. (This is when someone makes a rude comment about your act or tries to upstage you by being funny.) Daniels is a master at dealing with such remarks and coming out on top. His quick repartee and ability to think on his feet have helped him enormously in his career on television.

SERVAIS LE ROY'S

MAGICAL MONTHLY

No. 3.   AUGUST, 1912.   Gratis.

~ LEON BOSCO ~

~ The Comedy Wizard ~

Right ➤ This photograph from the cover of *Magical Monthly* magazine shows Leon Bosco, an early 20th-century magician, using physical comedy in his act.

The Characters Of Comedy

Secret Stooges

A stooge is someone who is secretly helping you as part of your act without the audience knowing. An example of a stooge is in the trick called the Friendly Trick (page 86).

Stooges can also be used to good effect to create comedy. One example is The Cut and Restored Tie. You need two identical ties. You get your stooge to wear one of them. You get him out of the audience and cut his tie in half, much to the amusement of everybody watching. There are various ways of restoring the tie at the finish. One of the most popular is a Change Bag, which is a bag that has a secret compartment in it. This can be bought from a magic dealer.

Another amusing situation is to get your stooge to hold a glass with no bottom. The audience thinks it is normal. You crack an egg into the glass and the egg spills all over his hand.

Sawing a Lemon in Half

An advantage of doing comedy magic is that you can entertain many people with only small props.

Emil Jarrow performed in huge theaters a trick very similar to the Copper Silver described in the Sleight of Hand section of this book (page 154). Most people could not even see the coins, but because he was so amusing it did not matter.

One of his specialty tricks was finding a borrowed bill inside a lemon that he cut open. At the height of the popularity of Sawing a Woman in Half in the 1920s, he was playing in a theater opposite Horace Goldin. The latter had a huge poster outside that read: "Come and see Goldin saw a woman in half." Jarrow put up a poster saying: "Come and see Jarrow saw a lemon in half."

Fred Culpitt

Inventing comedy tricks is hard to do. One man who was very successful at it was Fred Culpitt. "I don't want to cause any ill feeling...but I'm next!" was how he used to begin his act. He had a wide girth and made many humorous references to it. Behind the comic façade was an inventive mind and a gutsy performer. He would make a cane disappear by dropping it down a hole in the theater stage—he had sneakily drilled the hole himself the night before!

His best-known comedy trick was the gradual disappearance of a bathing suit from an attractive woman displayed on a canvas. With the audience anticipating she would end up naked, they couldn't help laughing when it turned out that the sea had risen to just below her chin.

Culpitt was different in a period when magicians tended to be relatively serious in their presentations. As a result, he successfully made the transfer from British theaters to variety shows where audiences wanted broader laughs. He died from a heart attack at the height of his career following the news that his grandchild had been killed in action during World War II.

Right ➤ Emil Jarrow performs "The Bill in Lemon" trick.

Big Magic

Magicians refer to big magic as illusions. Illusions, in magic parlance, are tricks that combine apparatus with people or large animals. The most popular illusion act is the male magician with his female assistant; although times are changing and more women are equal partners with their male counterparts.

Few magicians start off by doing big magic. Most illusionists, including David Copperfield, Lance Burton, and Siegfried Fischbacher (of Siegfried and Roy fame), begin with a manipulative act. Knowing how to perform with small magic helps you learn the necessary stagecraft to present illusions.

How Does Big Magic Work?

Presenting Illusions

There is a danger with big magic that the audience gives more credit to the clever apparatus than the skill of the magician. Because of this, although presentation is vitally important in all branches of magic, it is especially so with illusions. Music, staging, lighting, and choreography are all factors that have to be exactly right for large-scale magic to work properly.

One way of presenting illusions is in the form of a story. Possibly the greatest British magician was David Devant and one of his most famous illusions was the Artist's Dream. An artist is painting a picture but then becomes very tired and falls asleep. During the course of a vivid dream the painting he has been working on miraculously comes alive and the woman walks off the canvas and around the stage. The artist wakes up and tries to grab hold of the woman; but as he does so she melts away.

All Done with Mirrors

Many people like to think that most big magic is done with the aid of mirrors. There are some illusions where mirrors do play an important part. One of the earliest was the Sphinx where a live head sat on top of a table. The head spoke and could move but had no body. This was first performed in 1865 and caused a sensation. And it was all done with mirrors.

Another old and famous illusion, created around the same period, called Pepper's Ghost also uses a mirror. Here actors interact with a ghostly figure that appears and dematerializes at will. This is complicated to produce; as well as requiring a large mirror, the actor, who is playing the part of the ghost, has to be hidden in a pit in front of the stage.

Right ➤ An early illustration of the Sphinx trick delineates where the man's body still is beneath the table.

Read All about It

The number of great books on big magic are few and far between. One was written by David Devant in 1936 and was called *Secrets of My Magic*. Devant was expelled from The Magic Circle for a short period because parts of the book were reprinted in a magazine article. Another was Robert Harbin's own book, *The Magic of Robert Harbin*, which includes the method of doing the Zig-Zag Girl.

Undoubtedly the most peculiar was called *Jarrett Magic and Stagecraft*, written in 1936 by Guy Jarrett. Jarrett was a true eccentric. He never married and spent much of his life drifting around the United States. He had an unusual diet and was a lifelong believer that several times each day people should be turned upside down. It clearly worked for him because he lived to the age of 90.

His book combined brilliantly concise descriptions of some great illusions, together with very critical remarks about most contemporary magicians. One of his masterpieces was the production of no less than 21 women from a single cabinet. He had an unusual way of promoting the book, by saying, "Only a limited number of copies have been printed. Then after one month I will publicly burn all copies left."

Right ➤ The Disappearing Donkey was invented by the magician, Charles Morritt.

Far right ➤ Extracts from David Devant's *Secrets Of My Magic* got him expelled from The Magic Circle.

Big Tricks

Hiding the Elephant

It is rumored that when Harry Houdini once made an elephant disappear it took four people to push the empty box on the stage; and after the elephant had gone, 12 additional people to push the box off! Houdini was too good a performer to make such an obvious mistake but making animals disappear, whatever their size or temperament, is not an easy task for any magician.

One famous animal disappearance was invented by a British magician named Charles Morritt. The Disappearing Donkey was first performed in 1912. A witness was so impressed he thought the donkey had discovered a fourth dimension. Only recently has an illusion designer, Jim Steinmeyer, worked out how the disappearance took place.

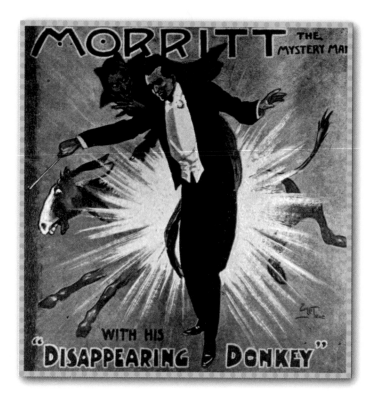

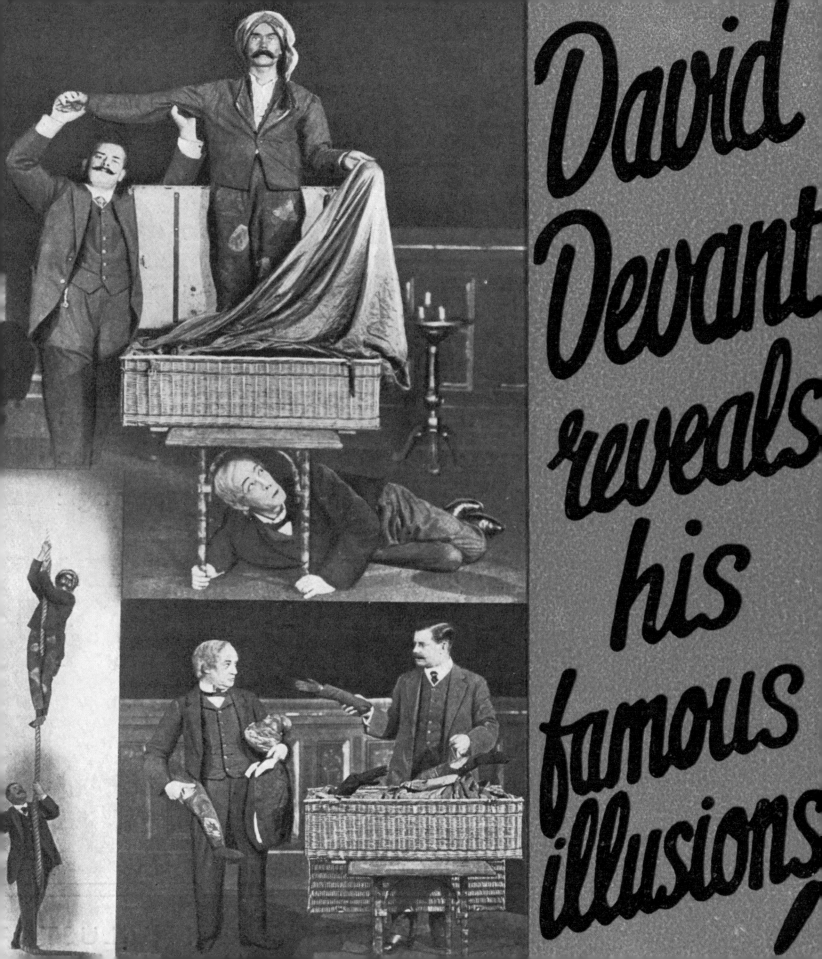

David Devant reveals his famous illusions

Levitations

Outside Sawing the Woman in Half, the most famous illusion is probably a Levitation. This is where somebody rises in the air without any apparent physical support. The first successful theatrical levitation was performed by J.N. Maskelyne, a great British magician who was the owner of two long-running magic venues in London from 1873 until his death in 1917. Particularly impressive was the passing of a solid hoop over the assistant while she was suspended in midair.

A great twist on the classic Levitation was invented by Servais Le Roy and is known as the "Asrah." Here the assistant is covered with a cloth and rises high into the air. The cloth is then whipped away and the assistant miraculously vanishes in midair.

The continual fascination with levitation is demonstrated by the sensation that David Blaine caused when he rose a few feet off the ground on his first television special.

A Cheap Illusion

Illusions are very expensive. This is because you are not only paying for the workmanship and material that go into the finished prop; but you are also paying for the secret. Here, however, is an illusion where all you need is a long piece of rope and a theater with wings. Wings are that part of the theater where you make your entrance and exit from the side of the stage.

The audience sees you walk from one side of the stage to the other, dragging something behind you on a piece of rope. Once you have exited, the rope continues to be pulled, then suddenly you appear on the other end. It turns out you have been pulling yourself!

You need two offstage assistants for this. One of them keeps the rope taut for you when you walk out onto the stage. When you have disappeared off the other side, your second assistant takes over the pulling. You quickly run around backstage to your original starting point and take hold of the rope from your first assistant. Wrap yourself around it and get the second assistant to pull you back onto the stage.

Left ➤ Demonstration of the "Asrah" trick.

Right ➤ The magician, Kellar, performing a levitation.

Masters of Big Magic

The Zig-Zag Girl

Illusions originally were built to perform in theaters. Most of them were therefore very heavy and bulky and not easy to transport. With the decline in theater shows, and the necessity for magicians to be able to work in smaller venues, lighter-weight illusions were required. Step forward pioneer inventor, Robert Harbin.

Born in South Africa he went to the United Kingdom as a young man. His most famous illusion is known as the Zig-Zag Girl. A woman stands upright in a box and her middle is pushed out to one side. It caused a sensation when it was performed at the famous London Palladium in 1965, however, it is also compact enough that it can be done in someone's living room. Furthermore, unlike some illusions, it is completely angle proof, which means you cannot detect the method wherever you are standing to look at it.

Box Jumpers

In some big magic the magicians do not have to do very much other than wave their hands and take their bow. It is their assistants who are doing all the real work. This might include squeezing into tight spaces and leaping out of boxes. This is why they are sometimes called box jumpers. Assistants can also add a great deal of glamour to a show.

Left ➤ Robert Harbin performing his most famous trick, the Zig-Zag Girl. The assistant doesn't seem too perturbed to be missing her middle!

Many assistants remain anonymous. One who did not was Moi-Yo Miller who assisted the great magician Dante. Dante was so famous in his time that he even had a starring role in a Laurel and Hardy movie. Moi-Yo was billed as Australia's most beautiful woman and became a vital ingredient in the show; she not only participated in many of the illusions but also helped to organize the details of the show backstage.

Many assistants end up marrying the magician. Famous husband-and-wife teams include Mark Wilson and his wife Nani Darnell who starred in their own television series for many years in the United States; and Paul Daniels and Debbie McGee who had similar success in the United Kingdom.

Great Illusionists

Traditionally in the United States there has always been one famous performer of big magic shows. The first of these was Harry Kellar who retired in 1908 and named Howard Thurston as his successor. After Thurston, who died in 1936, the best-known was Harry Blackstone, Senior. More recently, Doug Henning, followed by David Copperfield, have become household names.

Other illusionists traveled abroad rather than concentrating on one country. Carter the Great, for instance, made no less than seven world tours between 1907 and 1936. Dante, Cecil Lyle, and Nicola were others who toured the world with their show. After World War II such tours gradually ceased. This was partly because of rising costs; the amount of equipment and number of assistants that had to be transported was enormous. More important, the increasing popularity of movies meant less people were interested in live theater shows. The situation for magicians worsened with the arrival of television. Now, audiences were able to see equally impressive sights in the comfort of their own living room.

Quick Thinking!

Many people once had reason to thank the quick thinking of Harry Blackstone, Senior. He was once performing in a theater when a fire broke out backstage. Realizing that if the audience knew, they might start panicking, he announced he wanted to show everybody a spectacular new illusion, however, it was so large it would not fit inside the theater. He therefore wanted everybody to go outside so they could watch it in the street. The entire audience calmly walked out in single file and the theater was vacated—incredibly, without anyone being injured.

Breaking All Records
Largest Illusion

The biggest magic trick ever was the vanishing of the Statue of Liberty. This took place on national television in the United States and was performed by David Copperfield. The disappearance happened at night with a large crowd of people witnessing it. Although most of those present probably did not believe this national monument really disappeared, the illusion was nevertheless very impressive and it generated a great deal of publicity for him.

David Copperfield's other large-scale illusions include flying across the Grand Canyon and walking through the great Wall of China.

Copperfield's most talked-about big magic trick was probably the vanishing of a Lear Jet. Even though people were holding hands, and completely surrounding the plane, it still managed to disappear into thin air.

David Copperfield has the reputation of doing more live shows per year than any other performer. He continually tours all over the United States and is also hugely popular in countries such as Germany and Japan.

World's Fastest Illusion

Harry Houdini is famous as an Escapologist, however, he also invented a very impressive illusion that he called Metamorphosis. It is now better known as the Sub Trunk. The assistant is locked inside a trunk and the magician stands on top. He covers himself with a sheet; and when the sheet is lowered the assistant is standing there instead. The trunk is unlocked and the magician is found inside. Houdini performed this with his wife Bess. An updated version is performed by the U.S. illusionists, the Pendragons. They are a husband-and-wife team and very much a partnership. The transformation from one to the other on top of the trunk is conducted at lightning speed.

Right ➤ David Copperfield has been responsible for some of the most dramatic magic of modern times.

Silent Magic

Silent magic is magic where the performer does not talk. Although this can be true in many branches of magic, magicians refer mainly to silent acts as those that perform manipulation. This is the hardest magic to perform well as there is no opportunity to distract your audience with comments or stories. Instead, they have to try and retain the attention by continuous magical surprises.

Most silent acts perform for only a short period of time; 15 minutes would be considered a lengthy act. However the amount of magic that is packed in will comfortably exceed that performed by a talking act, lasting much longer.

Above ➤ An early book on magic shows how a
would-be magician could learn tricks.

Silent Magic in Action

Learning Silent Magic

A well-known silent magician wrote a book entitled *It's Easier than You Think*. Many who have read the book would choose to argue with the title. While some tricks do not require much practice, if you want to learn manipulative magic you need a great deal. To produce and make playing cards, silk handkerchiefs, and billiard balls disappear effortlessly takes not just hours but many weeks of committed toil. It is worthwhile time spent even if you decide to concentrate on a talking act. The techniques learned can assist you in all areas of performing.

Most magicians are self-taught. They teach themselves from books like this one and by picking up ideas from watching other performers, but if you want to be good at manipulation, you probably need a magical advisor. By acting as a third eye the advisor can assist you in finding ways of invisibly picking up your props so that it is not noticed by your audience. It's always a good idea to have another person watch you practice tricks before you perform in public as they will often notice subtle improvements that can be made to your tricks.

Gimmicks and Fakes

Magicians use many different types of props in their act. Some are exactly what they appear to be, for instance, playing cards and pieces of rope. Some, however, are not what they seem, or remain unseen. These are called fakes and gimmicks. Both are used extensively by silent magicians.

A fake is a piece of apparatus that looks normal but actually has some hidden secret unrecognized by the audience. A magician shows what seems to be a solid cane. He wraps it up in a sheet of newspaper, uncurls the paper, and the cane has disappeared. The cane, though, was not solid; it was a fake.

The best way to handle a fake is as you would handle something that is not fake. If it looks perfectly normal there is no reason why anyone should be suspicious of it. If you behave in a furtive way your audience will pick up on it and suspect something is wrong with the prop.

A gimmick is a secret device that is never seen by the audience. The silk handkerchief that disappears when placed inside the hand does not melt away into nothing; it has been secretly hidden away inside a gimmick. Gimmicks and fakes are most effective when combined with sleight of hand.

Tips for Performing Silent Magic

✳ **Record and watch your act back on a video camera. You will quickly spot any obvious mistakes which you might not pick up from looking in a mirror.**

✳ **Practice moving smoothly from one trick to another. Remember, you don't have any patter to fill empty spaces in your act.**

✳ **Choose any accompanying music carefully. It should complement the performance, not create attention away from the tricks.**

Silent vs. Patter Tricks

There are many tricks that can be performed either silently or with patter. An example is The Linking Rings, where solid rings of steel magically link and unlink. One of the greatest silent versions of this trick was performed by Richard Ross, a Dutch magician who won the FISM Grand Prix twice in 1970 and 1973. He used only three rings but it was performed so gracefully that the rings just seemed to melt through each other.

Another magic trick that is interchangeable between silent and talking is The Miser's Dream. Here, coins are produced out of thin air and dropped into a bucket. Although versions of the trick had been performed before him, T. Nelson Downs came up with the wonderfully descriptive title in 1895 and it instantly became a main feature of his act.

Teller, from the double act Penn and Teller, is well known for being mute. He performs a memorable version of The Miser's Dream where he produces coins and drops them into a fishbowl. At the end, the money all turns into fish.

Music for Magic

Silent magic is rarely completely silent—it is usually accompanied by music. The music is traditionally classical and without lyrics, but increasingly, with contemporary performers, this is changing. With the best acts the magic is timed to the music and matches the mood of what is happening on stage.

For instance, if you were to perform a trick such as The Diminishing Cards—an effect where a deck of cards gradually gets smaller and smaller—the music might start loud and then get quieter. With The Miser's Dream, the dropping of the coins into the bucket might be timed with the beat of a drum.

Some magicians have music specially written for them. Although expensive, this is the best option as it means you have no problem with copyright should you perform your act on television or in a public venue.

Dressing to Impress

The customary dress of the magician is a suit with tails. The main reason for this goes back to the silent act. The magician needs to hold the props, which he intends to produce, somewhere on his person. Having a jacket and long tails gives him plenty of places to hide the various objects. Today, this formal dress can appear rather dated, particularly if worn by young people.

Magicians have to find the right balance between looking contemporary and wearing garments in which they can easily carry their props. David Blaine performs in jeans and a T-shirt, but most of his tricks are done with only a deck of cards. If he had an act that produced many glasses of liquids, as the Polish magician Salvano has, he might have rather more of a problem!

Present-day silent acts have found a way around this problem, either by wearing special costumes or redesigning their act so they are not reliant on the traditional clothing. For example, the Swiss magician Peter Marvey manages to produce an endless stream of cards even though he is dressed in a sleeveless shirt.

Right ➤ A suit with tails was once the traditional dress for magicians. Modern-day magicians often prefer a more casual look.

Other Silent Magic

It is not just manipulative acts who perform silently; it is an important skill for any magician to acquire. For example, if you are performing magic in a very noisy environment or with loud music in the background, it is possible no-one can hear you speak, so it is good to have some tricks in your repertoire that can just be watched. Tricks in this book that would work well would include The Levitating Tumbler (page 77), Solid through Solid (page 132), and Cut and Restored String (page 74).

One magician who performed without speaking was Horace Goldin. He was born in Poland, so English was not his first language. He also had a trace of a stammer that made talking hard for him. Goldin was not the most graceful-looking man so manipulative magic would probably not have suited him. As a result, he mainly concentrated on a mixture of illusions and apparatus magic, all done silently and at great speed. He claimed to have performed no less than an amazing 45 tricks in 17 minutes.

Where to Perform

A great advantage of being a silent act is that you can perform anywhere in the world; language is not a problem. Theaters are probably the best places for silent acts—the lighting and staging are good, and audiences are fully attentive. Unfortunately, such venues are harder to find, which means silent acts have to be prepared to travel.

In recent years opportunities for work on cruise ships have increased. These are perfect for silent acts—audiences are international and of all ages.

Great Silent Magicians
And the Award Goes to...

Every three years there is the Olympic Games of magic, known as FISM. The most prestigious prize to win is the Grand Prix. The winner is usually a silent manipulative act. Perhaps the most famous Grand Prix winner is Lance Burton who won in 1982 in Switzerland with a superb act that was inspired by his hero Channing Pollock.

Channing Pollock revolutionized silent magic in the 1950s with his sultry good looks and his immaculate production of cards, silk handkerchiefs, and doves. As a result, he probably became the most copied magician in the history of magic. Lance Burton combined the production of candles with the other props. He also trained his doves so that when he produced them, they flew out of his hands onto a stand behind him.

Winning FISM set Lance Burton on the road to a full illusion show, which he now performs nightly in Las Vegas. However, he still opens each show with the same prize-winning act.

Left ➤ The Polish silent magician, Horace Goldin in performance.

The Greatest

It is hard to say who was the greatest magician ever; but in any top ten list one man would certainly feature. He was born Richard Valentine Pitchford in Wales but rose to prominence under the name Cardini. He learned his manipulative skills in the harsh environment of the trenches during World War I. Because it was desperately cold he had to put on gloves to practice. When he later developed his act, he therefore produced playing cards while wearing gloves.

Cardini mainly manipulated with cigarettes and cards, which in itself was not especially original. The reason he stood out from his contemporaries was because he played the timeless character of a tipsy gentleman. He therefore appeared as surprised as his audience as multiple cigarettes materialized, or cards sprung seemingly from nowhere at his fingertips.

When Cardini first began he used to talk during his act, but he discovered that his patter was distracting and took attention away from his superb artistry.

Cardini Meets Malini

Cardini for a time worked at a magic shop in New York. One day somebody came in and watched Cardini practice his card productions. The unknown person picked up a single playing card and it seemed to melt away in his hands. He showed his palms empty, his fingers spread. Cardini was staggered. He knew everything about card magic but this man had completely fooled him. Before he had time to ask any questions, however, the man had disappeared. All that was left behind was his business card, which read: You'll wonder when I'm here; you'll wonder even more when I'm gone. The magician who had fooled Cardini was called Max Malini, a brilliant close-up magician. It was the only time they ever met.

A Great Inventor

Buatier de Kolta was born in France but spent much of his performing life in England. He was arguably the greatest inventor in the history of magic. His most famous creation was an illusion in which a woman sits on a chair. She is covered with a sheet. In de Kolta's original version both the sheet and the woman disappear. This is commonly known as The Vanishing Lady but many magicians still refer to it as De Kolta Chair.

He came up with many tricks suitable for the silent magician. He was responsible for the popularity of sleight of hand with billiard balls as he thought up a clever gimmick to assist the manipulator.

A particular trick had fellow magicians completely perplexed for many years. This was the production of hundreds of flowers from a paper cone. They were amazed when they discovered they were actually paper flowers that sprung open. They were even more amazed to discover de Kolta had individually made every one himself!

Left ➤ The great silent magician, Cardini.

Women Magicians

Girls and women of course can perform all types of magic just as well as boys and men. Women, however, do tend to be more attracted to silent magic than other branches. One of the earlier women magicians was called Talma who worked as part of the three-person troupe of Servais Le Roy, Talma, and Bosco. She was a superb manipulator of coins and was known as the Queen of Coins.

Today there are many excellent women magicians and it is often fascinating to see how they reinterpret traditional magic. Tina Lenert performs an act in which she transforms herself from a cleaning lady to a beautiful woman in a dazzling dress. Chinese-born Juliana Chen is a juggler-turned-magician. In 1997 she won the first prize for manipulation at FISM, the first woman to achieve this prestigious title.

Joanie Spina is an example of what women can now achieve in magic. She began her career as an assistant to David Copperfield; and subsequently became his choreographer. She went on to star in her own show and now directs other magicians.

SERVAIS LE ROY'S

MAGICAL MONTHLY

No. 2   DECEMBER—JANUARY, 1911-12   Gratis

Mlle. TALMA

The Queen of Coins

Right ➤ Joanie Spina is a successful female magician.

Left ➤ In 1912 Mademoiselle Talma, featured here in *Magical Monthly*, would have been a rarity as a female magician.

Mind Magic

Mind magic involves picking up people's thoughts, anticipating how they will behave, and predicting the future. In today's world mind magic is the only type of magic that audiences often believe is real. There is still much unknown about the human mind and magicians take advantage of this in the presentation of their tricks. Magicians who specialize in mind magic are called mind readers or mentalists. Often they disassociate themselves from the world of magic. This is because if anyone suspected they might be using any magic-type props or sleight of hand their reputation as mind readers would suffer badly.

The Secrets of Mind Magic

Mind-Reading Tools

As a mind reader it is important you use only everyday objects that are familiar to your audience. Pieces of paper, envelopes, pencils, newspapers, and books are commonly seen in a mind reading act. If you use a deck of cards, then handle them naturally. Do not show any fancy cuts, shuffles, or other flourishes.

It helps if you have knowledge of phrases and words associated with mind reading; for instance, ESP, which stands for Extrasensory Perception, telepathy, clairvoyance, dowsing, tarot cards, numerology, palmistry, and cold reading. They are good to include in your patter to sound knowledgeable about your subject.

You can look, act, and dress slightly strange; that is almost expected if you are a mind reader. It is best not to wear traditional magician's clothes or use a magic wand.

Audience Participation

Nearly all magic uses audience participation; but none more so than mind reading. As one well-known mind reader once observed, "It would not be very interesting if I was to read my own mind."

Audience participation means involving people directly in the tricks. In other branches of magic this might be through getting someone to select a playing card that subsequently appears inside a wallet, or borrowing a bill that ends up inside a lemon. In mind reading it is more likely to be telling someone what playing card they are merely thinking of, or divulging the serial number on their bill.

Audience members you use in your magic are treated with respect. If you upset them, they are likely to cause you problems and the trick may be spoiled. Guidelines to achieve this are on page 46.

Right ➤ Newmann the Great was a popular mind-magic performer.

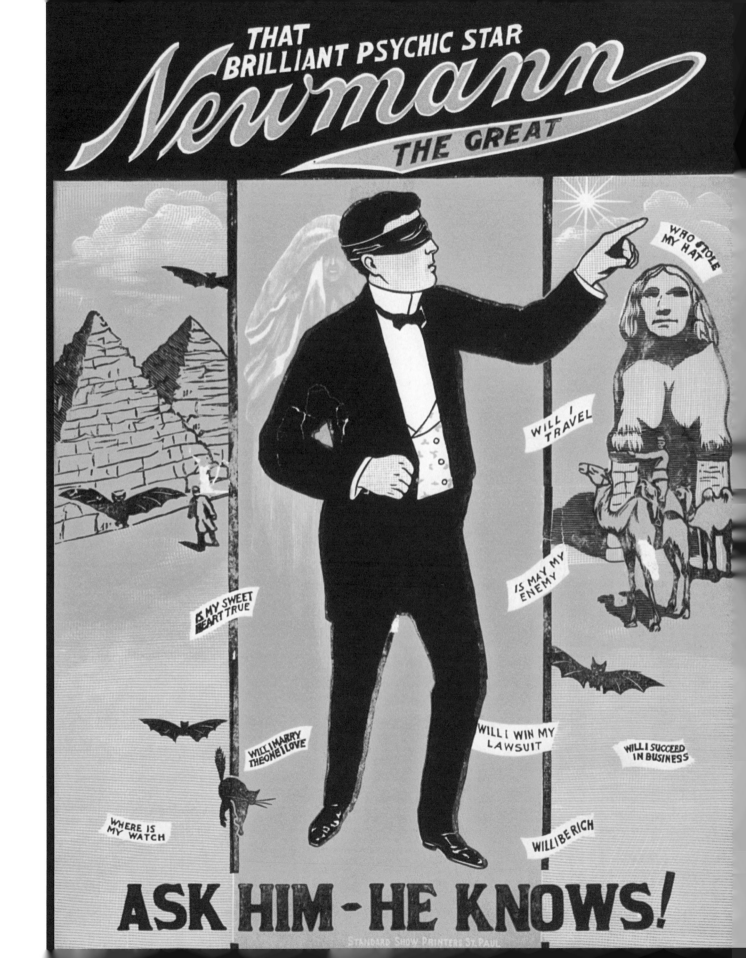

- Always ask their name and use it when speaking to them.

- Do not make them look stupid or make fun of them in an unkind way.

- Allow them to make the magic happen and to get some of the credit for the tricks working successfully.

- If you borrow anything, make sure it is returned in exactly the same condition.

- Thank them for helping and ask the audience to give them a round of applause at the end.

Deliberate Mistakes

Mind reading is one arena of magic where people can be impressed even when tricks go wrong. This is because if you could really read minds, it seems reasonable that occasionally you would make a mistake. For this reason mind readers often try out stunts that are not guaranteed to work. If they do succeed they seem really amazing. If they go wrong, they shrug it off as a near miss; and try something else instead. You might like to try these, which should work most of the time. Write down your predicted answers in advance on a piece of paper. Get someone to name a color. Usually they will say red. Ask someone to think of a flower—the chances are they will name a rose. Request them to draw two simple geometrical shapes, one inside the other. They will probably draw a triangle inside a circle. Alternatively it will be a circle inside a triangle. If that is so, point out you were nearly right.

Here is another experiment involving numbers. Ask someone to think of a two-digit number between one and 50. Both numbers must be odd and both must be different. You point out that 11 would be no good as, although both numbers are odd, both are the same. Write down on a piece of paper the number 35. Then cross it out and write down 37 next to it. Ask your helper to name the number. The chances are he will choose 37. If he selects 35, explain that was your original guess.

This works because the assistant actually has a very limited choice; the only numbers that fit the criteria are 13, 15, 17, 19, 31, 35, 37, and 39. For some reason, people very rarely choose a number in the teens. If it does not work, then try another trick that you know will succeed.

Humor and Mind Reading

Mind readers tend to be quite serious in their presentations. There is a good reason for this: they tend to be more believable. If you are continually telling jokes and making your audience laugh, people are less likely to think you can actually read their minds. Nevertheless, even during the most serious act it is always good to inject some humor.

Here is an example of some comedy mind reading. Ask someone to think of any word he likes. Meanwhile, you write down the word NO in large letters. Say to the person, "Yes or no, is there any way I could know what word you are thinking of?" They have to respond, "No." Turn around your prediction to show you are correct!

Right ➤ David Berglas achieved nationwide publicity for his impressive mind-reading stunts.

Mind-Reading Stunts

In order to advertise their shows, magicians enjoy performing one-of-a-kind stunts. If done well they can generate a lot of newspaper coverage and even exposure on television. The master of modern-day publicity is David Blaine who gained worldwide attention by sitting in a glass box for 44 days, being frozen in ice, and being buried alive.

Often, such events are of a mind-reading nature. A favorite is to predict the headline of a newspaper or the result of an upcoming sporting event. The envelope with the prediction inside is placed in a locked safe, or held securely by a well-known personality, to prevent any attempt at tampering by the performer. Despite this, the prediction is invariably correct.

Another popular stunt is a blindfold car drive. The mind reader is able to drive along a busy road, although his eyes are covered. David Berglas received extensive coverage in a prestigious magazine in 1953 when he combined a blindfold drive with the recovery of a lady's slipper hidden in a London park. It was this single amazing feat that propelled him to future stardom.

Claims to Be Real

Most mind readers rarely claim to be genuine as there is always a danger they might be found out. This happened to a brilliant mind reader named Maurice Fogel in 1949. He was pursued by a journalist when he made such an assertion and his methods were exposed. This was very detrimental to his career. Other mind readers have learned from this. Modern-day exponents, such as Derren Brown and Marc Salem, admit that an eight-year-old can copy what they do—with 20 years of practice!

Uri Geller, who is famous for bending spoons and starting broken watches, is a modern-day exception. He continues to maintain that his powers are authentic and no trickery is involved. Despite the attempts of magicians such as the skeptical James Randi to prove otherwise, there are still some who believe that Uri Geller has inexplicable powers.

Spiritualism

Uri Geller isn't the first person to claim genuine powers. Nineteenth-century Spiritualists maintained that they could communicate with those who have died, or that the dead could somehow speak through them. Spiritualists still work today and are sometimes known as mediums. Many people go to mediums to seek comfort when someone close to them has died.

Most mind readers are careful to distinguish themselves from mediums. Harry Houdini made it a personal crusade of his to expose mediums who were making false claims. He disagreed about this with his great friend, Sir Arthur Conan Doyle, the creator of Sherlock Holmes. Conan Doyle lost his son in World War I and sought the solace of mediums to communicate with him in the afterlife. He did not want to hear Houdini arguing that most mediums were frauds.

Right ➤ Uri Geller claims that his power to bend cutlery is down to authentic powers rather than trickery.

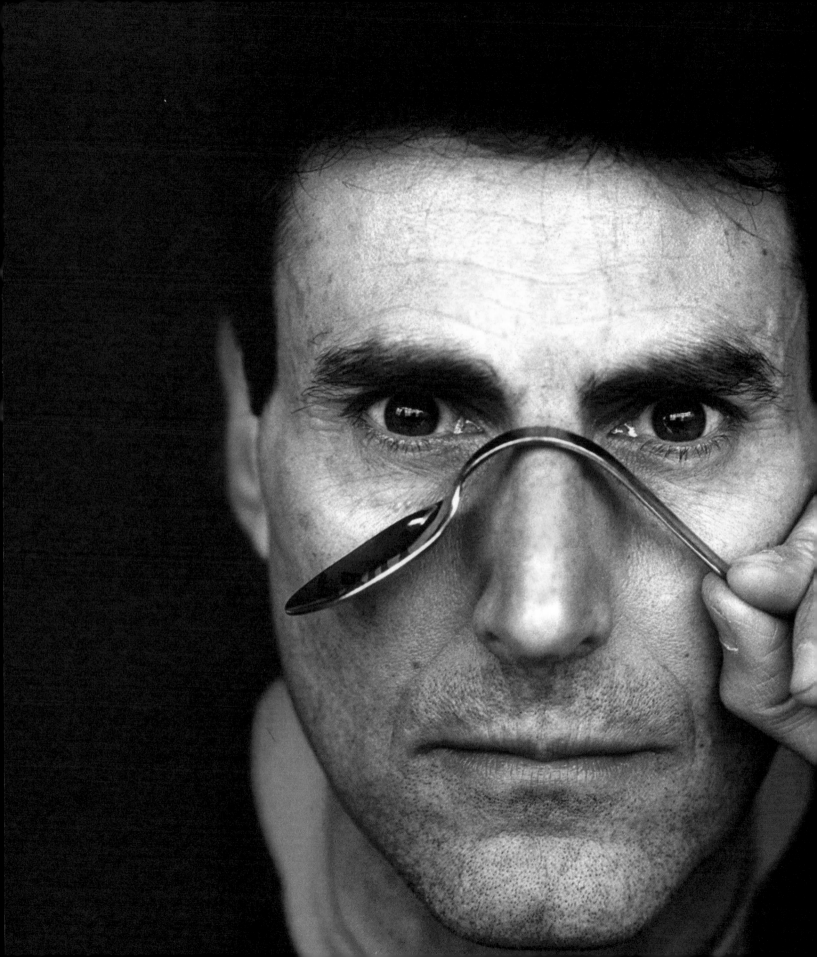

Mindful Magicians

Chan Canasta

Modern-day exponents of mind reading do not pretend they can actually read someone's mind. Instead, they say they are interpreting their body language, influencing people through subtle wording, and applying psychology to predict how they might react in any given situation. One of the first to cleverly exploit this was Chan Canasta, a Polish-born mind reader. He came to prominence in the United Kingdom with his own television show in 1959. He also appeared on U.S. talk shows.

Canasta mainly used playing cards to demonstrate his ability to manipulate his helpers. He repeatedly demonstrated how he could make people choose any card he wanted them to. His most famous stunt involved a book. Any word from any line from any page in any book would be chosen; and Canasta would reveal what it was.

Double Acts

Mind reading is very effective with two people. Demonstrations can be given of telepathy—where the thoughts of one person are picked up by another. One of the earliest exponents of this were the husband and wife team of the Zancigs, who used the byline: "Two Minds with but a Single Thought." Julius would borrow objects from members of the audience and his blindfolded wife Agnes would say what they were.

People suspected the two were using some sort of spoken code to communicate with each other, but even this theory could not apply to Sydney and Leslie Piddington who became a sensation in the United Kingdom a few years after World War II.

They did not talk at all and yet Leslie was still somehow able to pick up the thoughts of her husband. When asked if they used genuine telepathy their response was, "You be the judge."

Mind Reading on Radio

With mind reading the visual content is often minimal. It can therefore work on radio. It was through this medium that the Piddingtons, first in their native Australia and then in the United Kingdom, came to prominence.

The first major radio mind-reading star, though, was Joseph Dunninger. He had his own series in the United States in 1929 and again in the 1940s. He performed his mind reading on celebrities in front of theater audiences. Listeners could easily follow what was happening. Dunninger was a man of authority and this helped in convincing his listening audience that he could genuinely read minds.

Mind-Reading Books

The most prolific and influential writer on mind reading was undoubtedly Ted Annemann, who was born in 1907 in New York. As a performer he was not that successful, mainly because he suffered from dreadful stage fright. However as a creator of mind-reading effects and methods he was unsurpassed. He edited a magazine entitled *The Jinx*, which specialized in the subject. It had contributions from the top performers of the day. Tragically, in 1942 he committed suicide. Following his death his tricks were published in *Practical Mental Effects*.

Dangerous Magic

If you were a real magician, then you could risk your life on a daily basis and come out unscathed. This is why magicians perform dangerous magic—to demonstrate somehow that they are truly superhuman; however, it is the magician's job to give the appearance of danger. In other words, to make the trick look more perilous than it really is.

If You Dare to Perform

Learning Dangerous Tricks

The best advice about dangerous tricks is to not do them. There are many great tricks and there is no need to try anything where you may injure yourself. Remember, though, that even tricks that appear to be completely safe can have an element of danger in them. It is possible to cut yourself on a sharp pair of scissors when performing Cut and Restored String (page 74); or for the glass to shatter on the floor when doing Glass through Table (page 146).

The way to prevent accidents is not only by practicing a trick but also rehearsing it. Rehearsal is when you perform the entire trick from beginning to end. This means you know where your props are at the start, how you are going to get them out and put them away, and where they will be at the end.

For instance, if you want to carry a pair of scissors on you, they should not be lying in your pocket with the blades exposed; otherwise, when you reach into your pocket you could cut yourself. They should be put inside a tube or a special holder so that you can remove them with the handles.

Another rule that magicians follow to prevent any accidents is to always set up your props yourself—and do not let anyone else touch them.

A Dangerous Audience

A show's danger points aren't restricted to the stage. Many magicians earn a good living performing magic for five- to eight-year-olds at birthday parties and school events—and some say this is the most dangerous magic of all! This is because children tend to be much more honest if they think they have spotted how a trick works. Whereas adults are often too polite to say anything, youngsters will shout out what they think is the solution. To get around this, magicians perform "sucker" tricks. These are tricks where the magician appears to give away the secret, but it turns out that the supposed secret is just a hoax.

A well-known sucker trick is called the Dice Box. A die is placed in a wooden box that has two doors. The die appears to slide back and forth between the two, so when the magician opens one door, the die appears to be behind the other. Everyone shouts out for the magician to open both doors. But when they are opened, the die has disappeared. The audience have been well and truly suckered!

En spännande trollkonst.

På scenen står en stor kittel, fylld nästan ända upp till kanten med en vätska. Troll-konstnären sätter sig på bottnen, vätskan sluter sig över honom, och väldiga eldtungor slå upp över hans huvud; två element äro nära att uppsluka honom: skall han drunkna eller omkomma i elden? Efter en stund slockna lågorna, och till publikens förtjusning och häpnad reser sig trollkonstnären och hoppar upp ur kitteln utan att ha tagit minsta skada. Hur förklaras nu detta förvånande konststycke? Med få ord: trollkonstnären har övat sig i att hålla andan, så att han kan uppehålla sig ovanligt länge under vatten-ytan (det är nämligen vatten i kitteln). Lågorna framkallas av litet eter, som flyter ovanpå vattnet och som obemärkt antänts genom att man kastat litet kali däri. De båda vinjetterna nedtill visa ett annat trick, med vilket trollkonstnären väcker livligt bifall. Han inneslutes i kitteln, några av åskådarna lägga på locket och bomma till det, varpå gardiner skjutas för. När dessa en stund därefter dragas undan, står mannen bredvid kitteln, som fortfarande är förbommad. Hemligheten består däri, att de yttre reglarna

© S. & I.

From Canaries to Tigers

Performing with animals can be dangerous both for the animals as well as the magicians. A popular trick at one time was the disappearance of a live canary in a bird cage. The bird cage was held between the hands and in an instant completely disappeared, but many a canary was badly injured from broken legs or wings.

Even back in the late 19th century some magicians were sensitive to this cruelty. The great court entertainer Charles Bertram used to let the canary out of the cage before making it disappear. As the creature flew away he would say, "You have flown away, have you? Well, take the cage with you." Today, although the vanishing bird cage is still popular, no-one does it with a live bird.

The most dangerous animals that magicians work with are wild cats. These can be mountain lions or tigers. Many shows in Las Vegas feature these beautiful creatures. It must never be forgotten that while they are trained, they are never tamed, and the performers must be continuously vigilant to prevent accidents.

One of the first magicians to work with wild animals was the Great Lafayette. His most celebrated trick was The Lion's Bride, a playlet that involved a fully grown lion. Lafayette was a true lover of animals. He had a dog named Beauty, that was given to him by Houdini; he was crazy about his dog. A plaque at his home read: The more I see of men, the more I love my dog. His love of animals cost him his life. In 1911 a fire broke out backstage and in an attempt to rescue his horse, he died.

Left ➤ A poster from 1927 shows a stage magician being immersed in fire and water.

Right ➤ A shocked spectator pulls a magic wand from the magician's mouth.

Swallowing Magic

There are all sorts of ways of giving the impression of danger in magic tricks. One unusual, but very popular trick, is The Razor Blades. Here, the magician apparently eats a number of razor blades. He then breaks off a piece of thread and places that in his mouth too. One end of the thread is pulled from his mouth. Attached to it are the razor blades, all brought out in a neat row.

The trick was originally done with needles rather than razor blades and was a major item in Houdini's stage act. He would have his mouth thoroughly inspected before he swallowed the needles to show they could not be hidden anywhere.

Such a trick would seem to suit Houdini but it is performed by other magicians who do not court danger at all. For instance, The Razor Blades is a major feature in the act of the suave Hungarian magician, Paul Potassy. The Austrian magician Otto Wessely performs a comic version of the same trick; when he pulls out the thread there are dozens of razor blades attached and it stretches right across the width of the stage.

Tricks to Terrify

Catching the Bullet

There is one undoubtedly genuinely dangerous trick in magic. This is Catching a Bullet. It has claimed more than 12 lives. It is the one trick that Harry Houdini was advised by his great friend, the illusionist Harry Kellar, never to perform.

John Henry Anderson, a Scottish magician who billed himself as the Wizard of the North, featured the bullet catching in his act. He was nearly killed twice. The first time was when he toured the United States just after the Civil War. His audience in the South thought his billing was mocking them about their defeat, so they took some potshots at him!

Another time, an amateur conjurer assisted him with the trick and interfered with the gun so that it would fire a genuine bullet instead of a dummy one. Anderson was well aware of this but still took up his position and called out, "Now, sir, take a good aim at me—and fire! Fire, sir, fire!" The marksman did not have the courage and walked off.

The most famous death was that of Chung Ling Soo, who was killed in 1918 at a London music hall. Soo was not really Chinese but was an American magician named William Robinson. His version of the trick was a reenactment of how he had supposedly escaped death by firing squad when captured by Chinese dissidents. On this occasion it went tragically wrong because of corrosion in one of the guns used to fire the fatal bullet.

Sawing in Half

Selbit invented the single most famous trick in the history of magic. It is Sawing through a Woman, although it is better known now as Sawing a Woman in Half. Selbit, whose real name was Percy Tibbles, came up with the idea in 1920. When first shown to theatrical agents it was received with very little enthusiasm, but instantly became a big hit with the public.

Since Selbit's original there have been plenty of different versions. One of the most impressive is David Copperfield's Death Saw in which the magician cuts himself in half.

Selbit specialized in creating dangerous illusions; these included Crushing a Girl, The Elastic Lady, The Human Pincushion, and The Liquified Lady. It has been argued that these make-believe acts of torture were a reaction against the increasing freedom of women in society in the 1920s. It is more likely Selbit simply exploited to the fullest the age-old plot of the damsel in distress.

Selbit's most bizarre illusion was called The Wrestling Cheese. He challenged male spectators to wrestle a gyrating cheese to the ground. It was not a commercial success. Audiences preferred to see attractive women in danger.

Left ➤ Sawing a woman in half is one of the most enduring and famous dangerous tricks.

WAKE UP THE DEAD !

With Our New

"Sawing a Woman in Half"

AT LAST THE SENSATION IS COMPLETE

The one great feature that has not heretofore been acomplished, or even dreamed possible, **is now the paramount issue. It is simply this:** After the box has been severed in half, and the two portions separated as far apart as desired, the front doors of both sections are opened, and the **lady shown absolutely in two parts.** You say it cannot be done. That's exactly what we say of any other version in the world but ours, and in which only one lady is used.

This illusion, complete this way, will cost you just $375.00 in special traveling crate. Delivery in 10 days

THAYER
MFG. CO.
334 S. SAN PEDRO
STREET
LOS ANGELES
CALIFORNIA

The Magicians Who Dare to Be Dangerous

Myth of Houdini

The most famous magician for doing dangerous tricks was undoubtedly Houdini. His feats included escaping from icy rivers and being buried alive. He had an instinct for catching the public's imagination with his stunts. He was the first magician to escape from a strait jacket and developed the gruesome sounding Water Torture Cell Escape. In this trick his feet were manacled and he was held upside down in a glass cabinet full of water.

Houdini, however, was rarely in any serious danger. He took immense precautions with all his escapes and made sure that if a trick did go wrong he would be rescued by an assistant. His death did not occur while performing a trick but was the result of his overconfidence. He claimed that he would feel no pain if hit in the stomach. Somebody backstage at a show punched him without warning. He refused to see a doctor before it was too late; and died, on Halloween day in 1926, of a burst appendix.

The Discoverie of Witchcraft

The first Western book containing a magic section was *The Discoverie of Witchcraft* written by Reginald Scot in 1584. Scot wrote the book because he was horrified by the treatment inflicted on witches which included putting them to death. He set out to prove that any feats supposedly performed by witchcraft could be done by magic tricks. The book gave explanations for some extremely dangerous tricks. These included how to thrust a knife through your arm and to cut half your nose asunder; and to cut off ones head and to lay it in a platter. Similar tricks are still performed today. They come under names such as Knife through Arm, the Finger Chopper and the Guillotine. However they are usually presented in a comical rather than a serious manner.

Left ➤ An advertisement selling Sawing A Woman In Half to magicians.

Right ➤ An illustration from *The Discoverie of Witchcraft*, originally published in 1584. In the trick, the magician's head appears to be on a platter.

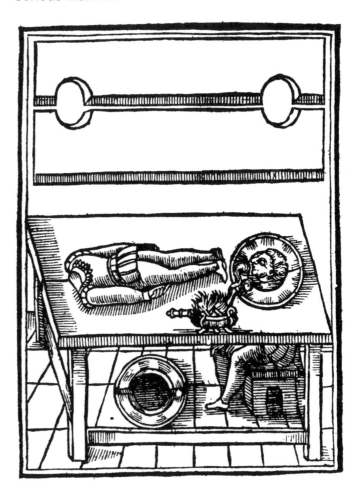

Contemporary Performers

Contemporary performers continue to perform perilous tricks. Many of these are on television so it is difficult to tell how dangerous they are. Robert Gallup jumped out of a plane handcuffed and locked inside a crate. He had to free himself, get out of the crate, and put on a parachute before he hit the ground. Lance Burton was tied on the track of a roller coaster ride and just escaped before he would have been hit. As he said afterward, "That was stupid."

Derren Brown, of the United Kingdom, gained a lot of publicity by performing a version of Russian Roulette. He was accused by the media of using blank bullets rather than live ammunition. But as he pointed out, even blanks can cause considerable damage when fired at close range.

Hans Moretti, a German magician, performs genuinely dangerous tricks all the time, and does not rely on any assistance from television. One of his most celebrated is firing a crossbow behind his back while blindfolded. In homage to the famous William Tell story, this is aimed at an apple perched on his wife's head. He also places himself inside a cardboard box and wooden poles are thrust through it from every possible angle. Somehow he manages to avoid injury and comes out of the box wearing a completely different costume.

Penn and Teller

This magic duo have the reputation of performing extremely dangerous magic. Teller has been run over by a giant truck and is nightly drowned inside a water tank. Penn has had his hand repeatedly stabbed. They have performed tricks with venomous snakes and insects—they always survive unharmed.

Even more risky, they have incurred the wrath of magicians by exposing certain secrets of magic. They perform a version of the classic Cups and Balls with transparent cups, and demonstrate the principle of trapdoors by repeating a stage illusion, originally done with opaque boxes, with clear acrylic boxes. Most sensible magicians realize, however, that the principles exposed by Penn and Teller can still be exploited in their own performance without any danger of audiences discovering the secret.

Above ➤ Penn and Teller are two successful modern-day magicians who are known for their dangerous magic.

Left ➤ Houdini was an inspired performer and self-promoter, as this poster shows.

Floating Ruler

This is one of those tricks that seems so simple you wonder why anyone is taken in. If performed well it will be talked about far more than other tricks that require a great deal of practice.

1 Place a ruler on the palm of your right hand just below the fingers. Hold your right wrist with your left hand.

2 Place your right thumb on top of the ruler so it is gripped and then turn your right hand face down. In the same movement extend your left index finger so that it is underneath the ruler.

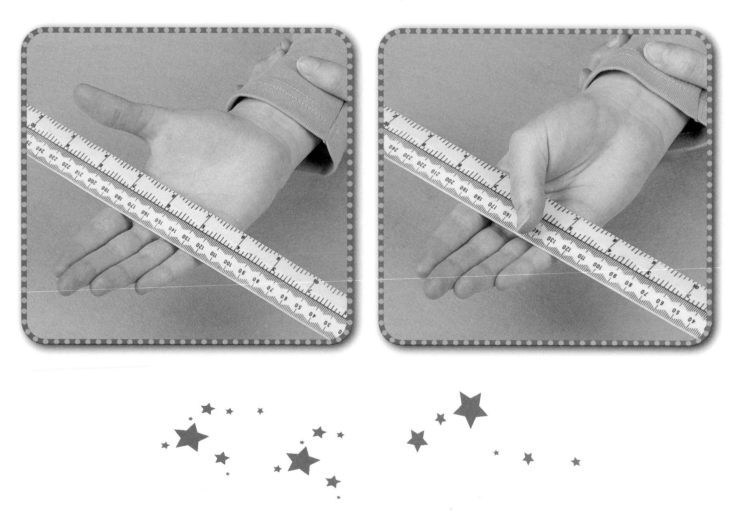

3 Keep your hand flat to conceal your index finger and bring your right-hand thumb away, so your hand is fully spread and the ruler appears to float.

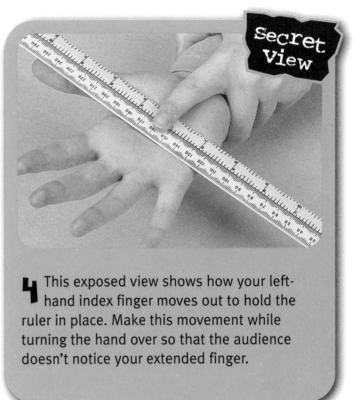

secret view

4 This exposed view shows how your left-hand index finger moves out to hold the ruler in place. Make this movement while turning the hand over so that the audience doesn't notice your extended finger.

Extra Tips

✶ You want to make this trick appear very difficult. Talk about how, with intense concentration, you can make objects stick to your fingers. Stress that it does not always work but you are prepared to give it a try. You can make your right hand "tremble" with the effort of keeping the ruler floating. If you want, put the ruler down, take a few deep breaths, and then start again. Do not hold the position for too long and finally, draw back the extended finger a little so the ruler drops to the floor, as if you are exhausted.

Magic Compass

Here is a trick that is fun to make and easy to perform. To make it you need a 2-inch (5-cm) square piece of cardboard. The color of the cardboard can be the same each side or, as in the photographs, different.

1 On each of the four sides of the square mark where it is about one inch from each corner. Then draw a diagonal line between each mark. Cut along the four diagonal lines to make an octagonal-shape compass.

3 Hold the compass at A and E between your index finger and thumb. Swivel the compass around 180° and draw an identical arrow, pointing in the same direction, on the other side. This is also between D and H.

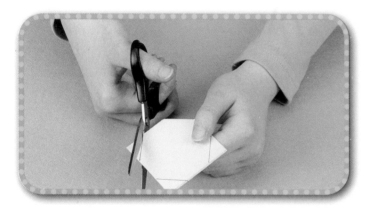

2 Draw an arrow on one side, as in the photograph, from point D to H.

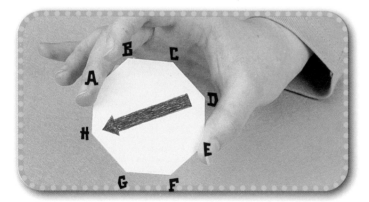

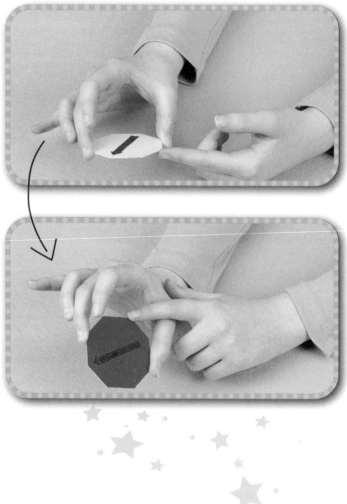

4 Shift the compass around so you are holding it at point B with your finger and F with your thumb. The arrow is pointing downward.

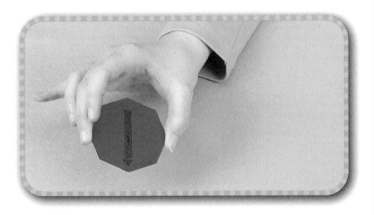

5 This time, when you swirl it, the arrow appears to rotate 90 degrees.

6 Turn it back again. Finally, shift the compass so you are holding it at points C and G. The arrow points diagonally down to your left. Now when you rotate it, the arrow points in completely the opposite direction.

Extra Tips

* The best way to present The Magic Compass is to construct a story. Explain how you were trying to find your way to the park. It seemed very straightforward: all directions were pointing in the same way. You demonstrate by holding the compass at A and E and swiveling it around.

* As you are talking, shift the compass to B and F. Having walked a little further, you discovered there were two possible paths to take. Either to your left—indicate where the arrow is pointing now. Or straight ahead—rotate the compass to show the arrow's new direction.

* As you were confused you decided to take your own route. Shift the compass between C and G. Unfortunately, you got completely lost as it turned out the park was in the opposite direction. Turn the compass around to show where the arrow is pointing. So you ended up abandoning the trip and going home!

Flying Cards

Here is a real classic of card magic. Many versions involve palming but this relies more on subtlety. Apart from a deck of cards you also need an envelope. The envelope must be larger than a playing card.

1 Place three of the cards underneath the envelope. Position them at the edge of a table so both the envelope, and the cards underneath it, are overlapping. This needs to be done without anyone noticing.

Secret View

2 Hand the deck to your helper and tell him to count ten cards face down onto the table.

3 As he is reaching the end of his count, pick up the envelope with the three cards underneath. Because they are overlapping the table, they are easy to pick up. The cards are hidden from your audience.

4 When he has finished his count, place the envelope on top of the pile. This secretly adds three cards to his pile of ten cards.

5 Ask him to check that the envelope is empty.

6 He places all the cards inside and seals it.

7 Pick up the rest of the deck and tell everyone you will attempt to make three extra cards end up inside the envelope. Make some magical gestures or sharply riffle the deck of cards in the direction of the envelope.

8 You can have some fun by asking your helper if he felt any of the cards arrive. Tell him to tear open the envelope. Inside he finds 13 cards.

Extra Tips

✳ When you pick up the envelope with the three cards underneath, everyone should be watching your helper count the cards. So if you accidentally show the cards no-one should notice.

✳ Casually toss the envelope on the pile of cards. If you place it down too neatly it looks suspicious.

Bluff Book Test

This is a simple version of a classic trick known as a book test. It comes from the brilliant mind of David Hoy. It can be done anytime with any two books you have to hand.

1 Ask someone to choose a book. Take it from him and flick through it.

2 Stop at a page near the middle and remember the first word at the top of the page. Also remember the page number (assume it is page 98).

3 Give his chosen book back to him and pick up any other book.

4 Explain that as you riffle through this second book, he is to call out stop wherever he likes. Start riffling through the book. The book is held toward you so nobody else can see the page numbers.

5 When he shouts stop, open the book, and look at the page number. Call out page 98 and then close the book.

6 Tell him to open his book at page 98 and remember the first word on the page. Of course you already know what it is.

7 Ask him to concentrate on the word. Rub your own forehead in pretend concentration. After enough combined concentration, tell him what the word is.

Thumb Fun

There are not many tricks you can do with just your bare hands. Here are a couple where first, the tip of your thumb is removed and then the thumb is magically stretched.

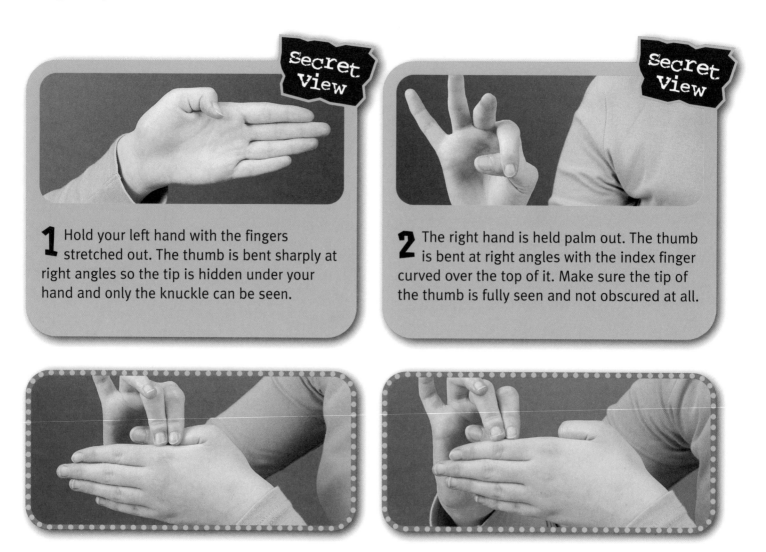

1 Hold your left hand with the fingers stretched out. The thumb is bent sharply at right angles so the tip is hidden under your hand and only the knuckle can be seen.

2 The right hand is held palm out. The thumb is bent at right angles with the index finger curved over the top of it. Make sure the tip of the thumb is fully seen and not obscured at all.

3 Place the right thumb tip next to the knuckle on the left hand. The right index finger and middle finger conceal the join where each thumb knuckle is bent. The illusion is created of a single thumb.

4 Slide the right hand along the left hand, apparently removing the thumb tip.

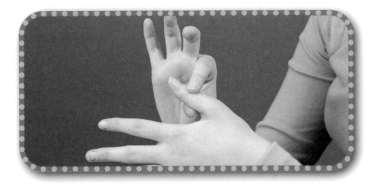

5 Return to the starting position. The left thumb straightens out and is gripped at the joint between the right index finger and thumb. At the same time move both your hands quickly up and down to cover this action.

Secret View

6 To create the illusion of stretching the thumb, tuck the right thumb under the first two fingers of the right hand. All the fingers are curled in. The tip of the thumb protrudes from between the two middle fingers.

Secret View

7 Push the left thumb under the first two fingers of the right hand so the two thumbs are aligned. Make sure none of the left thumb sticks out. The left-hand fingers are stretched out.

8 Move the right hand upward, stopping just before the left thumbnail is revealed. It looks like your thumb is much longer.

Extra Tips

* Practice getting in and out of the correct finger and thumb positions with no hesitation. Although nobody will believe you have genuinely removed or stretched your thumb, both illusions are extremely deceptive.

Cut and Restored String

Cutting and restoring a piece of rope is a favorite trick of magicians. It is equally impressive using a piece of string. You also need a pair of scissors. Handle them carefully as you do not want to cut your fingers.

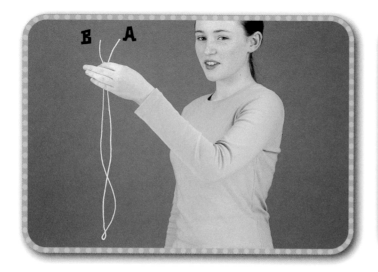

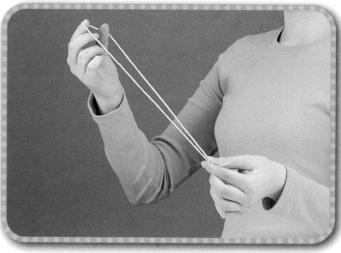

1 Begin with a piece of string about 4 feet (1.2 m) long. Let it hang down from your left hand, holding the string between your fingers and thumb. Bring the other end of the string up level so it is also held in the same position, side by side. One end is A, the other B.

2 Place the index finger and thumb of your right hand in the loop in the middle of the string.

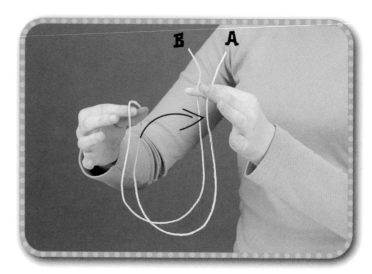

3 As your hands come together, pinch the top of B, with your right-hand finger and thumb, just below the left-hand fingers and thumb.

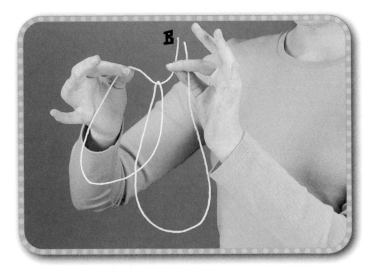

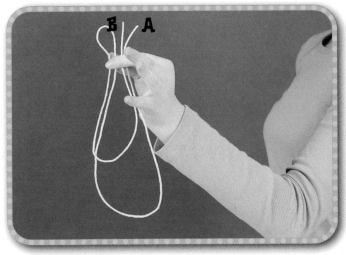

4 Without hesitation continue upward forming a new loop with the end of B. In the process the middle of the string hangs off the bottom of this new loop.

5 Your left-hand finger and thumb pinch all these pieces of string together so that it appears you are holding the middle of the string, in a loop, next to ends A and B. However, the loop is actually just the end of B; the original middle of the string is concealed by the fingers.

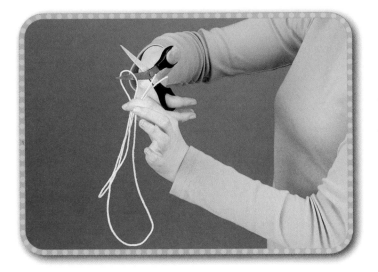

6 Pick up your pair of scissors and cut the loop in half. Put the scissors away, as you need both your hands free.

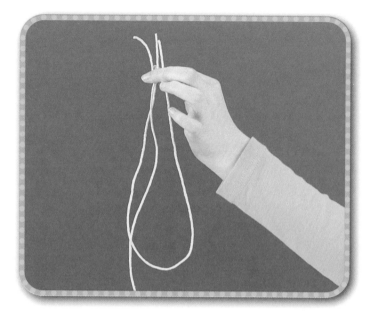

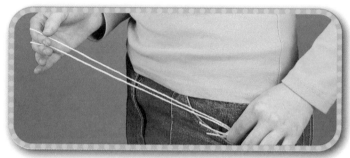

7 With your right hand begin by pulling down the end of the string farthest away from you. Then release the end of the string nearest you, leaving you holding a small piece of string hooked onto a long piece of string. The place where they join together is still concealed by your left-hand finger and thumb.

8 Take hold of the bottom ends of the pieces of string with your right hand. Place the other ends held by your right hand into a pocket. As your hand goes into your pocket, push the short piece of string so that it is unhooked from the longer piece.

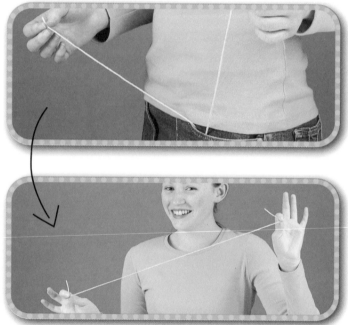

Extra Tips

✳ Practice this in order to see how it would look if you were about to really cut the middle of the string. It should look the same as creating the extra loop.

✳ Even though the string is slightly shorter at the end of the trick, this will not be noticed by the audience.

9 Once the short piece is removed, take hold of two ends of the long piece of string in each hand. Pull them apart and the string comes out of the pocket fully restored.

Levitating Tumbler

There is a well-known trick in which a glass is held upside down on a book. This uses a special gimmick. In this version all you require is some tape but it is just as effective. The clever idea comes from Robert Harbin.

1 Cut off a piece of tape 1¾ inches (44 mm) in length. Fold ½ inch (13 mm) back on itself. This leaves ½ inch (13 mm) of doubled-over tape and ¾ inch (19 mm) of sticky tape.

Extra Tips

✶ Place a handkerchief inside the glass. A little corner can rest underneath the tape. The tape will not be spotted, even close up.

✶ When removing the handkerchief from the glass at the end, peel off the tape as well. This leaves no evidence.

2 Stick the ¾ inch sticky tape to the bottom inside of your glass. The double fold is bent so it is on the outside.

3 Place the glass on a book. Press your thumb down on top of the folded tape. The rest of your fingers are gripping under the book.

4 Keeping your thumb pressed down, you can turn the book sideways. The glass appears to be stuck.

5 Continue turning the book over until the glass is upside down. At the end, simply remove the glass.

Through the Glass

One popular prop used by magicians is called a silk (a fine silk handkerchief). You need two. You also need a small straight glass. One of the silks must fit inside the glass without falling out when it is upside down.

1 Hold the glass at the bottom between your middle finger and thumb. Place one of the silks in the glass.

Secret View

2 Pick up the second silk in your left hand and cover the glass. Out of sight, allow the glass to swivel upside down by releasing the pressure with your right finger and thumb.

3 Adjust the silk so that it neatly covers the glass.

4 Your hands swap over so the left hand holds the glass.

5 Showing your right hand empty, go underneath the silk and pull out the other silk from the glass. It should look like you have pulled the silk through the bottom of the glass.

6 Your right hand goes back under the silk and holds the glass by its rim, once again between the middle finger and the thumb. Take hold of the silk at the top with your left hand and start to lift it off.

7 Under cover of this, let the glass swivel back so that it is the right way up.

8 Take the silk completely away to display the glass upright.

Extra Tips

✻ You will have to find the right-size glass to easily swivel around your fingers. Also be sure of your angles when you drape the silk over the glass. It is best if your audience is in front of you.

✻ To make the trick appear harder, cover the top of the glass and the silk with a rubber band. Although of course this will actually be the bottom of the glass as unknown to your audience, it is upside down.

Boxes and Balls

This is a variation on the classic trick "cups and balls." You need three boxes, large enough for your hand to be hidden when it is placed inside. You also need three sets of three identical small balls, each of a different color.

1 Place the three sets of colored balls in front of their respective boxes.

2 Pick up a black ball and pretend to put it inside the black box, but actually keep it. It is held out of sight by the curved third and fourth fingers.

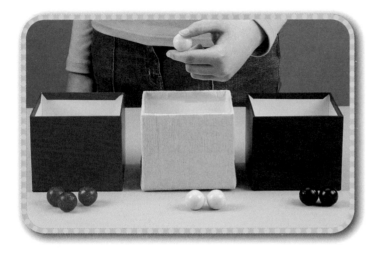

3 With the same hand, pick up a yellow ball with your index finger and thumb. Pretend to drop that in the yellow box but actually drop the original black ball.

4 Under cover of the box, the yellow ball is rolled across to be held as before by the third and fourth fingers. The hand appears empty.

5 Pick up a red ball and secretly drop the yellow ball in the red box. Again, the red ball is concealed in the third and fourth fingers.

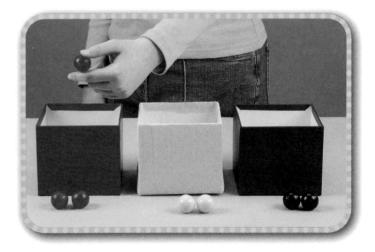

6 At this stage there are no balls in the black box, a black ball in the yellow box, and a yellow ball in the red box. You have hidden in your hand one of the red balls.

7 Pick up a black ball and drop the red ball in the black box, retaining the black ball.

8 Pick up a yellow ball and drop the black ball in the yellow box. Then pick up a red ball and drop the yellow ball in the red box You have three balls left with a red ball concealed in your hand.

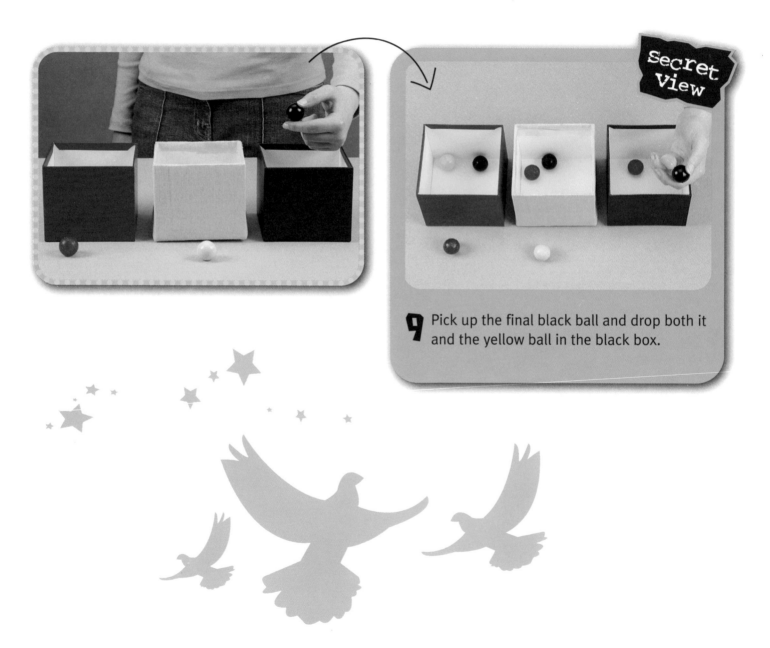

Secret View

9 Pick up the final black ball and drop both it and the yellow ball in the black box.

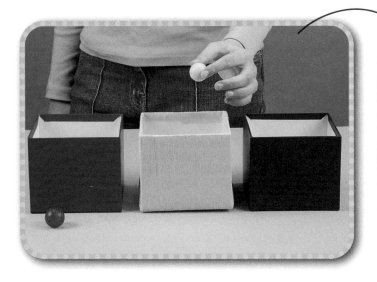

10 Drop the final yellow ball in the yellow box and the last red ball in the red box.

Extra Tips

✴ To perform this trick well you need to get into a good, steady rhythm. There should be no hesitation as you drop each ball into each box.

11 Your audience thinks each box contains the three matching colored balls. Tip the three boxes up to reveal a black, yellow, and red ball in each box.

Matching Cards

You will even fool yourself when you perform this trick. It comes from the inventive genius Paul Curry. It is best presented with two helpers—a boy and a girl. They should be friends.

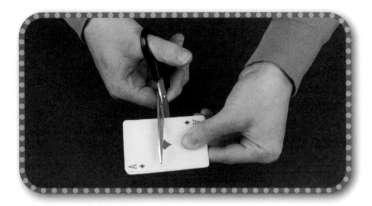

1 Allow the two friends to choose any five playing cards from a deck. Take the cards and cut them all neatly into two.

2 Place the two piles next to each other, one face up, the other face down.

3 Instruct the girl to move a half-card from the top to the bottom of the same pile. She can choose either pile. She is to repeat this three more times, switching back and forth between piles any time she likes. Or she can stick to the same pile throughout.

4 Explain that the reason for doing it four times is because there are four letters in "girl."

7 Ask the girl if she thinks she will remain friends with the boy when she grows up and becomes a woman. She will say, "yes." Tell her to move five half-cards this time, as that is the number of letters in the word "woman." Again the top two half-cards should be placed on the table.

5 When she has finished, take the top half-card of each pile and place them on the table next to each other. One will be face up, the other face down.

6 Get the boy to repeat the procedure. He is to do it three times as there are three letters in the word "boy." Again the top card of each pile is placed down on the table next to each other and in front of the first two cards.

Extra Tips

✳ So long as the first time four half-cards are shifted, the second time three half-cards, then five, and finally three again, the trick automatically works. Therefore, if you want to try a different presentation, you can alter the words you are spelling. Just make sure the new words have the appropriate number of letters.

8 Ask the boy if he thinks he will remain friends with the girl when he is a man. He moves three half-cards for the word "man." Place the top two next to each other. The remaining two half-cards are left where they are.

9 Turn over the first two face-down half-cards to show they match the face-up half-cards. "You are obviously good friends now," you say. Turn over the next two half-cards—"You will obviously be friends when you grow up." Turn over the final half-card: "Clearly you will be friends for life."

Friendly Trick

Tricks using accomplices are not usually recommended. It restricts when you can perform them and you never know if your helper might reveal the method. But this trick is worth the effort and risk of a secret assistant.

1 Openly place a ring, coin, or any other small object in the center of a handkerchief. Hold it through the handkerchief at the top with your right-hand fingers and thumb.

2 Flip your hand over so that the ring is covered by the handkerchief. Ask several people to check that the ring is still there. Do not lift the handkerchief up with your left hand to expose the ring. Instead make sure that their hands go underneath the handkerchief to feel the ring.

3 Finally, ask your accomplice to check that the ring is still there.

4 She should go underneath the handkerchief in the same way but this time she removes the ring from your hand. You still hold the handkerchief in the same position as before, as if the ring is still there.

secret view

5 Take one corner of the handkerchief with your other hand. Let go with your right hand and let the handkerchief drop. Pick up another corner of the dropped handkerchief with your right hand and show it on both sides. The ring has gone. Your accomplice can pretend she is amazed!

Extra Tips

✳ Try and practice with your helper removing the ring a few times before performing it for an audience. Your fingers and thumb should not move at all as she takes the ring.

✳ There is no need for her to try and palm it. As soon as her hand leaves the handkerchief, turn away and ask everyone else to watch carefully. This means that people's attention will shift from your accomplice. When she sees no-one is watching her, she can put the ring in her pocket.

✳ Do not be too quick to show the disappearing ring once it has gone. Use time misdirection to delay the disappearance as long as possible.

Time Please

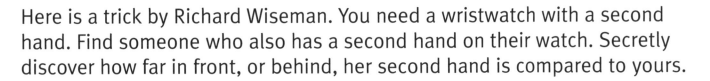

Here is a trick by Richard Wiseman. You need a wristwatch with a second hand. Find someone who also has a second hand on their watch. Secretly discover how far in front, or behind, her second hand is compared to yours.

1 Glance at the other person's watch and see where her second hand is pointing. Immediately check your own and calculate how many seconds they are apart. It does not have to be exact; to the nearest five seconds is good enough.

2 Assume when her second hand is pointing at 8, yours is at 5. This means the difference is plus 15 seconds. Remember this figure.

3 Ask her to think of any number from 1 to 12. She is to look at her watch and when the second hand passes that particular number, she should say, "Now."

4 Turn your back on her, explaining that you do not want to have any chance of seeing her watch. Look at your own watch.

5 When she calls out "Now," simply add three to the nearest figure from 1 to 12 that your second hand is pointing at. Three, of course, is equivalent to 15 seconds. Say she calls out when your second hand is next to the figure 2. This means she is thinking of the number 5.

6 Amaze her by revealing this.

Extra Tips

✴ This obviously works best if the person has no idea you even looked at her watch. Remember, you can delay doing this trick for almost any length of time. Ask someone the time one day, calculate the difference, and do not perform the trick until the next day. You can even do it over the telephone!

Rising Matchbox

This type of trick is sometimes known as an icebreaker. In other words, it is fun to do to attract the attention of people you want to perform magic for. You need an empty box of matches.

Extra Tips

✶ The initial trapping of the skin may take a little practice. You have it correct when the tray is closed around the skin and the box does not spring open.

✶ To cover the time you are taking to trap the skin, tell your audience you are trying to balance the box on the back of your hand. When you have the skin trapped, proudly display the box flat on your hand as if that is what you were trying to do. Your audience will not be impressed. At that point you can start making the box rise so it is balanced on one end.

1 Place the box upside down on the back of your hand with the tray partly out. Your fingers are stretched out flat.

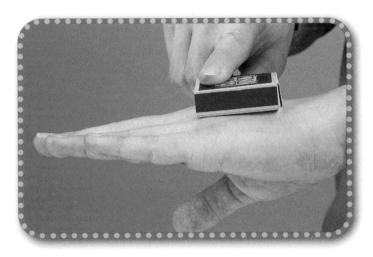

2 Close the tray, trapping a little bit of your skin between the outer box and the tray.

3 Slowly curl your fingers in. The box of matches rises to a vertical position.

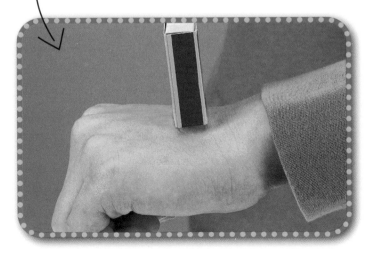

Extra Tips

✳ Keep the attention focused on the box of matches and wave your other hand over the top. This misdirects anyone noticing the fingers curling in. The slower you make the box of matches rise, the more impressive it looks.

Loop the Loop

There are many tricks with rubber bands. This is one where two instantly change places. Begin with two bands of contrasting color. Assume one is green and the other red.

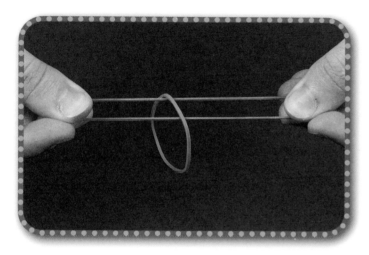

1 Place the red band through the green one. Hold the red band in your two hands so the green one hangs off it.

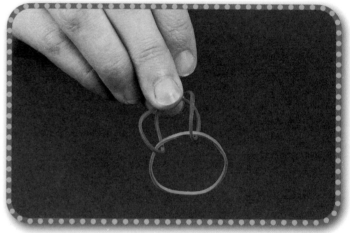

2 Double over the red band and hold it at the top between your right index finger and thumb. The green band still hangs off it.

3 Place your left thumb through the doubled-over red band.

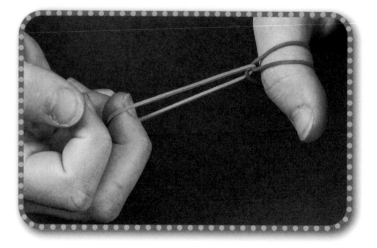

4 Hook the bottom of the green band with the middle finger of your right hand. Tug it up and down, stretching the band in the process.

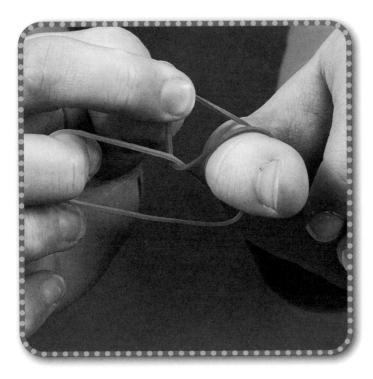

5 As your hand goes up and down, pinch any part of the red band between the index finger and thumb of your right hand.

6 As soon as you have seized the red rubber band, you can release the green one from your middle finger.

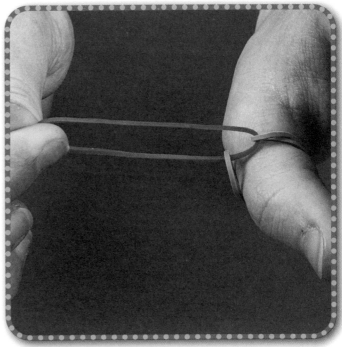

7 Quickly pull down the green band with the index finger and thumb. In the process the two bands change places.

Extra Tips

✻ To maximize the effect, emphasize at the start the position of the green and red rubber bands. As you pull on the green band it looks impossible for them to change places.

Coin in Glass

People are often deceived in magic by sound, as well as sight. Here both these senses are tricked. You will need a small, clear glass, a coin, and a handkerchief. You also need a rubber band, which is in your pocket.

1 Drape the handkerchief over your left hand. Place the coin in the center of the handkerchief, pinched between the left index finger and thumb.

2 Hold the glass in the palm of your right hand.

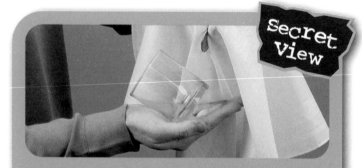

Secret View

3 Bring the handkerchief over the top of the glass as if you are about to drop the coin inside it. In the process the handkerchief covers the glass and your right hand.

4 Under cover of the handkerchief, gently push the glass back at a 45° angle with your right-hand fingers.

Secret View

5 Release the coin. It hits the side of the glass and falls into your right hand. Lower the glass again so it is lying on top of the coin.

6 Remove the handkerchief to show the coin is inside the glass; actually it is under the glass.

7 Cover the glass again.

9 Wrap the rubber band around the handkerchief at the top of the glass.

secret view

8 Lift the glass and the handkerchief off your right hand. Your right hand goes to your pocket, leaves the coin behind, and removes the rubber band.

10 Wave your hand in a magical gesture. Whip off the handkerchief to show that the coin has disappeared.

Extra Tips

✳ As your hand goes to your pocket to remove the rubber band, keep the back of your hand toward your audience. Try not to close your fingers; the coin should just be resting on them. Don't rush.

✳ It is important to say in advance that you need a rubber band. Otherwise, it looks suspicious if you suddenly go to your pocket without a reason.

✳ The noise of the coin hitting the side of the glass convinces people it is inside.

Quick Escape

Many escape tricks can be quite dangerous. However, this one is very safe and quite easy to perform. You will need an assistant, a handkerchief, and a piece of rope.

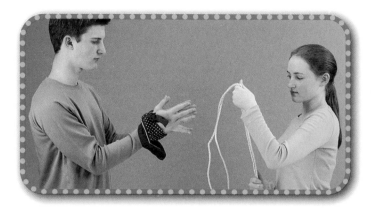

1 Have your wrists tied together with a handkerchief. You do not want them tied too tightly, so stress that you do not want your blood circulation cut off! In preparation, your helper picks up a piece of rope.

2 The rope is then placed between your arms and looped over the handkerchief. The two ends of the rope are stretched out in front of you by your helper.

3 Have another person cover your wrists with a coat or large scarf.

Secret View

4 Request that the helper holding the ends of the rope pulls tight. This enables you to grip the rope with the heel of your hands. Under cover of the coat or scarf, start working the center of the rope toward your fingertips.

5 When you have worked the rope far enough forward, bend the fingers of one hand inward. Tuck them underneath the rope and push the hand through.

6 Pull your hands back so the rope slips down next to the knuckle on the outside of your wrist.

7 Tug sharply to release the rope from the handkerchief.

Extra Tips

✳ Having first gripped the rope between the heel of your hands, you may need some slack to work it under the handkerchief. Tell your helper not to pull the rope too tight.

✳ If you practice enough you may be able to escape from the rope without covering your hands with a coat or scarf. You will need to turn sideways to do this, to prevent people from seeing how it is you actually escape.

Torn and Restored Napkin

Magicians perform many tricks where they tear up different types of paper and restore them: for instance, newspapers or money. Here you need two paper napkins, each around 8 or 9 inches (20 or 23 cm) square.

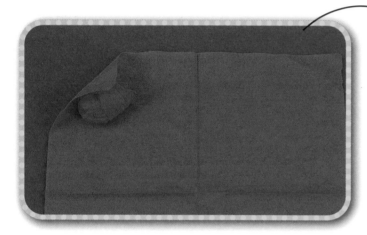

1 Prepare a set of napkins as follows. Roll a napkin tightly into a ball. Place this on the corner of another napkin and wrap it up a little.

2 Place the set in your pocket or somewhere else you can conveniently take it from.

3 When you are ready, pick up the napkin, unroll it and hold it spread out. The extra napkin is hidden behind it.

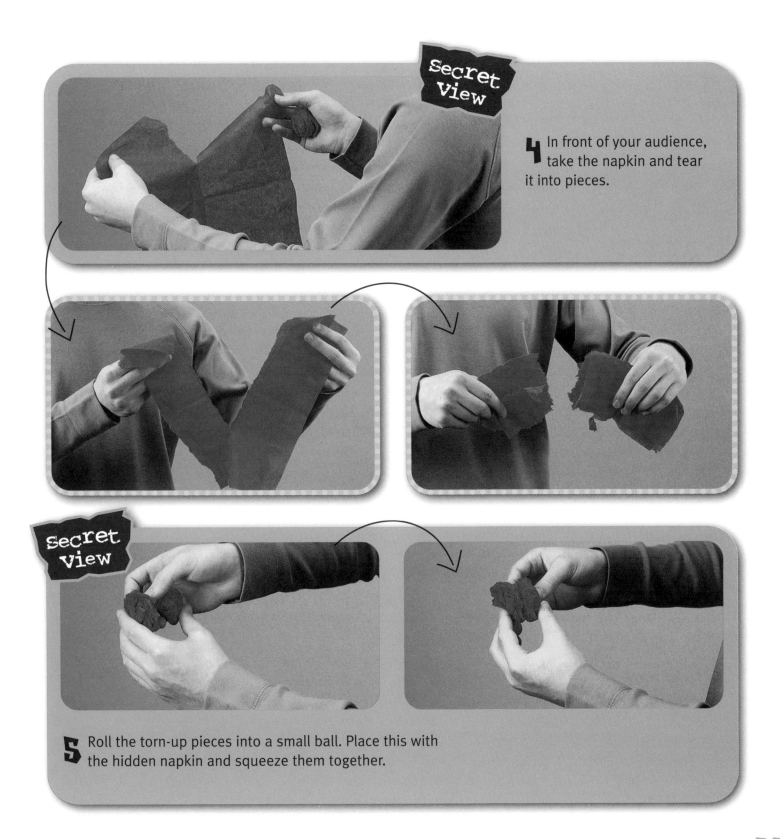

4 In front of your audience, take the napkin and tear it into pieces.

5 Roll the torn-up pieces into a small ball. Place this with the hidden napkin and squeeze them together.

the big book of magic fun **99**

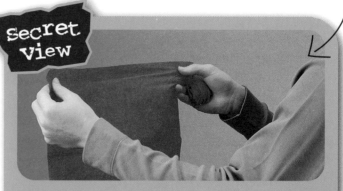

6 Unfold the second napkin, keeping the torn-up pieces concealed behind it during the process.

7 Display the "restored napkin" to your audience, keeping the rolled up torn pieces hidden.

Extra Tips

✳ It might seem that concealing an extra napkin in your hand is hard. However, at all times you are openly displaying one napkin, which makes it easier to hide another. Also, when you squash two napkins together, nobody can tell there is more than one.

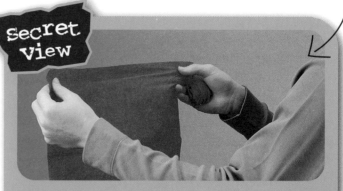

Paddling Knife

One of the oldest and most deceptive sleights in magic is known as the paddle move. It is best taught separately before showing a trick that can be done with it.

The Paddle Move

You can learn this with a cutlery knife although you may need to experiment a little to find one that is suitable. It is better if the handle is slightly rounded rather than flat.

1 Hold the knife with your right-hand fingers with the thumb resting on top.

3 To execute the paddle move you need to duplicate this action. However as you turn your wrist inward, your finger and thumb twist the knife over 180°. The handle of the knife is revolved by pushing your thumb outward and pulling your index finger inward.

2 To show the other side you would normally turn your wrist inward, keeping the same finger grip.

4 The end result is that you actually show the same side of the knife at the finish of your wrist turn. By reversing the move you are back to where you started.

5 The paddle move is done smoothly, without jerking. Do not try to hurry the actions too fast. If it is kept at an even pace, it is completely deceptive from all angles.

Knife and Paper

Apart from the knife you need two small squares of paper, similar in size and shape, torn from a newspaper or napkin. They must fit on the knife without overlapping the edges. To affix the squares on the knife, you need to wet them.

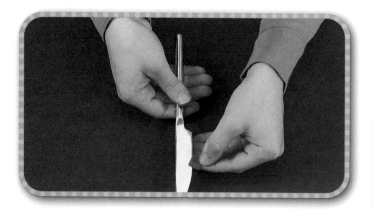

1 Place a piece of paper on one side of the knife.

2 Show the other side of the knife, using the same actions as the paddle move without actually doing it. Point out that there is one piece on one side and none on the other.

3 Turn the knife over and place the second piece of paper on the other side in the same relative position. Again show both sides.

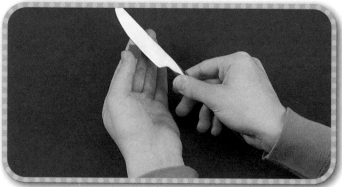

4 Remove the top piece of paper by resting your thumb on the top and pulling it off. Hold it between your left thumb and index finger.

5 Ask the question: "If I remove one piece, how many does that leave?" As you say this, pretend to chuck the piece you have removed on the floor. You actually keep it between your finger and thumb.

6 Again, duplicating the paddle-move action, show that the knife has only one piece on it now.

7 Turn the knife over as if you are dumping the remaining piece of paper into your left hand. At the same time turn your left hand underneath the knife to reveal the previously held piece of paper. Your audience thinks this is the second piece of paper.

8 Ask the question: "If I remove the other piece, how many does that leave?" As you say this, throw away the piece of paper that you have in your left hand. Whatever the answer, do the paddle move to show the knife has no paper on either side.

9 Tap the knife on a glass, or another solid object, a couple of times.

10 On the third tap revolve the handle around your fingers. This is the finger actions of the paddle move without the wrist turn.

11 Pause and show that one piece of paper has returned. Then do the paddle move to demonstrate that both have now reappeared.

12 To finish, remove the single piece left with your finger and thumb as you did before. It looks like you are taking off both pieces of paper together. Chuck this on the floor.

Extra Tips

✳ Carry out all your actions slowly and deliberately. This makes the reappearance of the two pieces of paper that much more impressive.

✳ Ask your question at the same time as you pretend to throw the first piece of paper on the floor. This misdirects your audience from looking for the paper.

Taking a Bow

Here is a great impromptu effect that can be done almost anywhere. You need a rectangular piece of paper that is 7 x 1½ inches (17 x 3 cm) wide.

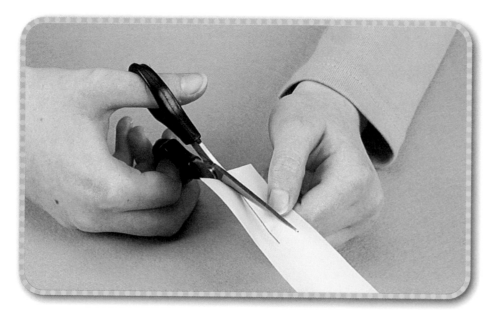

1 Fold the paper in half lengthwise. Unfold the paper. Tear or cut, 2 inches (5 cm) of the paper lengthwise along the fold from the bottom.

2 Refold the paper and you are all set.

3 Hold the paper by your index finger and thumb just below the top of the tear. By moving your thumb very slightly downward, the paper bends at right angles just above your thumb. To present this, pick up an imaginary thread and wrap it around the top of paper. Pull the thread with the other hand.

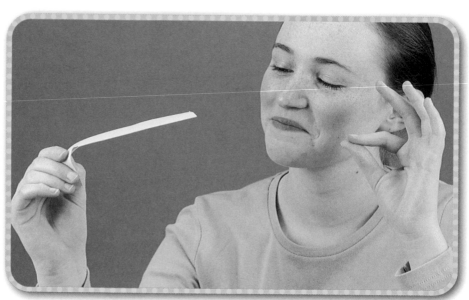

4 Let go of the pretend thread with your other hand and, by shifting your thumb back upward, let the piece of paper spring back up to attention.

5 At the end, tear the paper up to show there is nothing concealed inside. This destroys the evidence of the prepared tear.

Extra Tips

✶ This works with thin paper as well—such as a sheet of newspaper. Secretly prepare the paper in advance by making your 2-inch (5-cm) tear. You can then pick up the newspaper and go straight into the trick.

✶ If you are having difficulty making the paper bend, then slightly wet your thumb. This provides sufficient drag on the paper to make it bend.

Number Confusion

Misdirecting an audience comes in many forms. Sometimes it is possible to do it by words alone. This is one trick where you must use the exact wording suggested to make it convincing.

1 Ask someone to cut a number of cards from the top of a deck. You do the same—just make sure that you cut off more than he.

2 Ask him to secretly count how many cards he has; you do the same. Suppose you have 18 cards.

3 Say you will make three statements that are true. First, "I have the same number of cards as you"; second, "I have two additional cards"; and third, "I have enough cards left over to make your total sixteen."

4 Make up any low number in your second statement—it could be one, three or four as well as two. You then subtract that number from the number of cards you are holding and use that as the number in your third statement.

5 Ask him to place his cards in a pile on the table. Ask him how many he has. Assume he has seven cards.

6 Deal seven cards from your pile on the table next to his, proving you have the same number of cards as he.

7 Discard two of your cards, representing the two extra cards in your second statement.

8 Then count the remaining cards in your pile on top of his. The first card you place down you count as eight; the final card is 16.

9 Your three statements are true. You have shown that you knew how many cards he had cut.

Extra Tips

✶ This works automatically providing you take at least a few more cards than he. This means he must not cut off more than half the deck.

✶ It is important you use the exact wording as written above. The second statement confuses the listener. He does not appreciate that you are only really saying that your extra cards added to his total cards will equal your total cards—which of course is always true if you have more cards than he!

✶ Unlike most tricks, this can stand an instant repetition. Just change the numbers in your final two statements.

Banana Split

Any trick with fruit is always fascinating to people. This is one that requires some advance preparation but is worth the effort. You need a banana and some needle and thread.

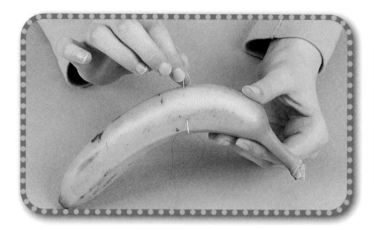

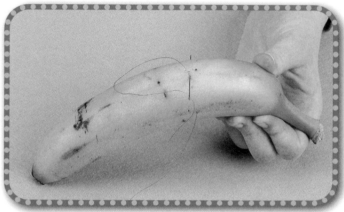

1 Push the needle with the thread through the skin of the banana and bring it out the other side. The needle runs along the side of the banana avoiding the fleshy part you eat.

2 The needle is brought back through the same hole and pushed out further around the banana.

3 This is repeated a few more times. You want to completely encircle the inside of the banana peel with the thread.

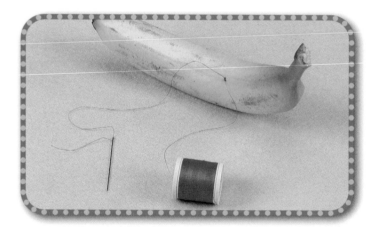

4 Finally, thread the needle through the first hole you made.

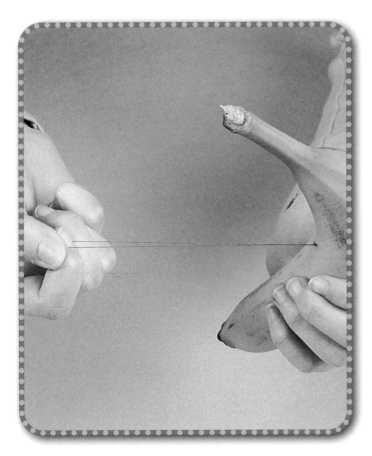

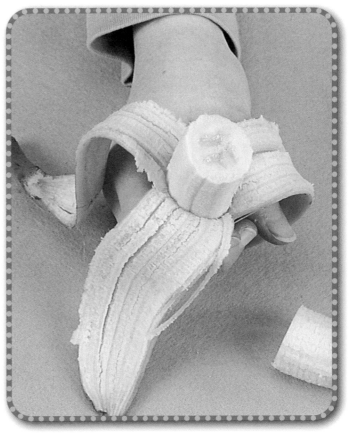

5 Pull the two ends of the thread completely out. This cuts the banana in half inside its peel.

6 If done correctly there should be no evidence of any damage to the outside peel of the banana.

7 When the banana is peeled it will be cut in half.

8 A way of performing this trick is to tell your audience you can perform a psychic karate chop. Demonstrate by bringing your hand swiftly down on top of the banana without actually touching it.

9 Ask someone to peel the banana and watch their amazement as the banana falls apart as the skin is unpeeled.

Extra Tips

✳ It is possible of course to precut the banana into several pieces. You can then have several psychic karate chops.

✳ This trick is even more impressive if you casually remove the banana from a bunch.

Bangle and Ribbon

Here is one of the few tricks where the magician uses the sleeve. You need a piece of ribbon around 2¹/₂ feet (76 cm) in length and two identical bangles. You need to be wearing an item of clothing with long sleeves and a pocket.

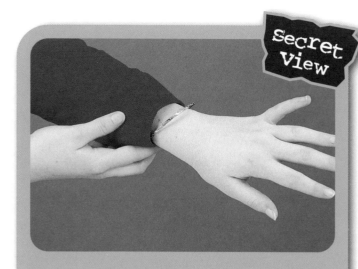

Secret View

1 Begin by placing one of the bangles tucked out of sight up your sleeve. This bangle will not be seen by your audience.

2 The ribbon is tied around your wrists.

3 Pick up the bangle and state that you will try and get it on the ribbon.

4 Turn your back on the audience and place the bangle in a pocket.

5 Pull the other bangle down your sleeve onto the ribbon.

Extra Tips

✴ Turning your back on your audience is not normally a good idea as you lose eye contact with them. So practice this trick so it can be done as speedily as possible. Try to minimize your arm movements.

✴ If you can, perform another trick before this one with the bangle up your sleeve. This is more likely to throw the audience off the scent of how the trick is done. It probably needs to be above your elbow so it does not accidentally slip down.

6 Turn around to reveal that the bangle has materialized on the ribbon.

Quick Release

This is a clever puzzle that you turn into magic by a little bit of cheating. You need a continuous loop of string about 3 feet (91 cm) long. The string is going to have to slip easily through a buttonhole.

1 Thread the loop through one of your own buttonholes. Place your two thumbs at either end of the loop.

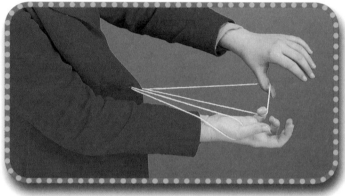

2 Make sure the string is not twisted. Bring your hands together, keeping the string taut. With your right little finger hook that portion of the string just above your left thumb. Grip onto it and do not let it go. You might find it easier if you pinch it between the little and third finger.

3 Hook your left little finger over the equivalent portion of string just above your right thumb.

4 You are now holding the string in four places; hooked around your two thumbs and two little fingers. Separate your hands.

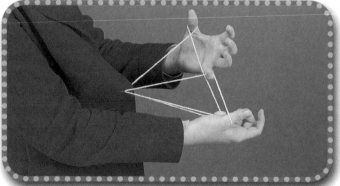

5 Draw the string back and forth through the buttonhole, all the time keeping your little fingers and thumbs hooked around the string.

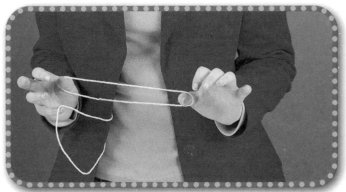

6 Slip your left thumb out of its loop and place it in the same loop as your little finger. When you have done that, remove your little finger.

7 At the same time, release the string from the little finger of your right hand. The string is once more held by just your two thumbs.

8 By slowly pulling them apart the loop of string comes out of your buttonhole.

Extra Tips

* The shift of your thumb out of one loop and into the other is covered by the larger movement of shifting the string back and forth.

* Present this as a challenge. You are going to remove the loop from your buttonhole; but at no time will the loop of string leave your thumbs. Anybody else trying it will find it impossible.

Coins Across

Here is a classic trick where the coins go across from one hand to another. Normally this requires some advanced sleight of hand. This method uses subtlety instead.

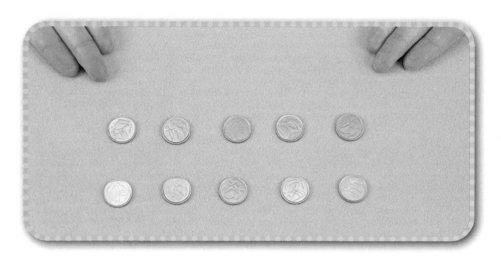

1 Begin with ten coins on the table. They should all be of the same denomination.

2 With the left hand pick up two of the coins. As you do so, say out loud, "Two coins."

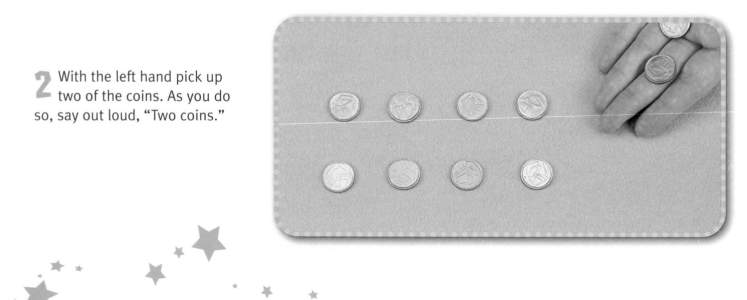

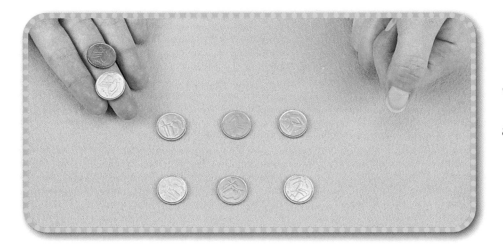

3 With the right hand pick up another two coins. Once again say, "Two coins."

4 The left hand picks up another two coins. Repeat "Two coins." The right hand picks up another two coins. The left hand picks up the final two coins.

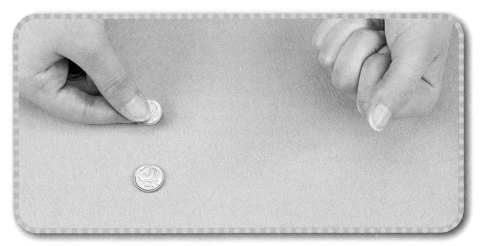

secret
view

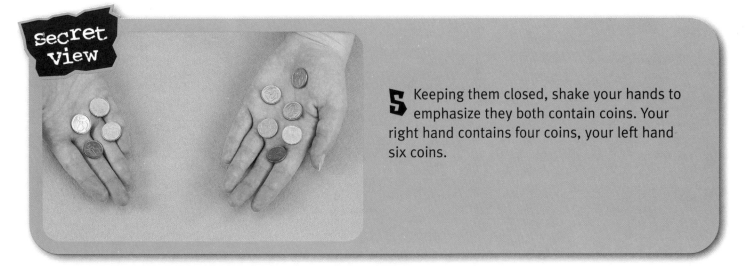

5 Keeping them closed, shake your hands to emphasize they both contain coins. Your right hand contains four coins, your left hand six coins.

6 With the right hand place two of the coins on the table. As you do so, be careful not to show how many coins there are in your hand. Say, "Two coins."

7 Place two coins from your left hand down. Again make sure nobody can see how many coins the hand contains. Say, "Two coins."

8 Put the last two coins from your right hand on the table. Make it look like you still have some coins left in that hand. Say, "Two coins."

9 Holding your closed two hands outward, look at your left hand and say, "Two coins." Look at your right hand and repeat, "Two coins."

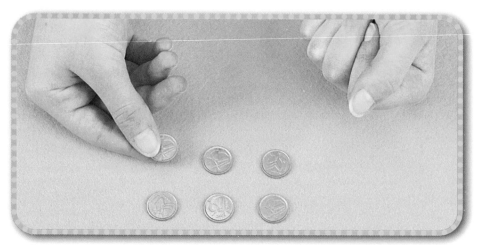

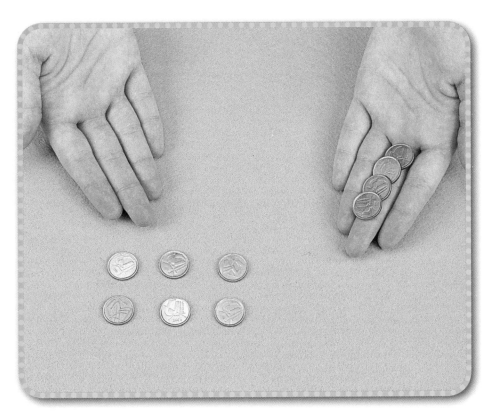

10 Slowly open your right hand and show it is empty. Tip four coins from your left hand onto the table.

Extra Tips

✱ This trick works partly because of the repetition of the words: "Two coins." It draws attention away from the fact that one hand holds four coins and the other six. Try and keep a continuous rhythm of picking up and putting down the coins.

Jumping Toothpick

This is the perfect trick to really get your friends going. You need two toothpicks. Claim the trick is done by static by rubbing one of the toothpicks on your sleeve.

1 Hold one of the toothpicks at one end gripped between your thumb and index finger of your left hand. The toothpick is held horizontal and points inward.

Extra Tips

✴ This might take a little time to get the knack. You need to exert a lot of pressure against the left-hand toothpick; the finger and thumb push inward, while the index fingernail pushes outward.

✴ The downward movement, or scraping, of the fingernail against the toothpick is tiny and cannot be seen by anybody watching. As a result it looks as if the toothpick leaps in the air on its own.

2 The toothpick rests on the nail of your middle finger.

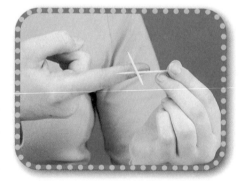

3 Place the second toothpick on top of the first at right angles to it. It balances on the toothpick and the middle finger of your right hand.

4 Gripping the left-hand toothpick tightly, press it firmly against the fingernail. Now if you move your fingernail down, the second toothpick jumps up.

Slot-Machine Hand

All that is required here is a single coin; it is therefore hard to beat as an impromptu quickie. By using a larger the coin, you will find this trick easier to perform.

1 Hold a coin in your right hand at your fingertips. Place your left hand so that it is palm down with the fingers curled inward. Place the edge of the coin on the back of your hand.

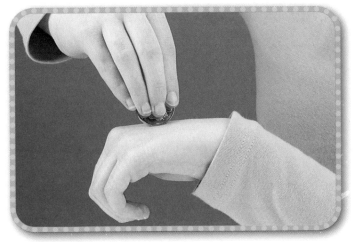

2 Begin to slide the coin backward and forward. At the same time, push down with your right-hand fingers so they begin to cover the coin.

3 When the coin is about halfway covered, freeze your right hand. Turn your left palm up and explain that the coin eventually should come out the other side.

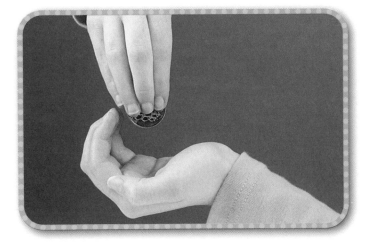

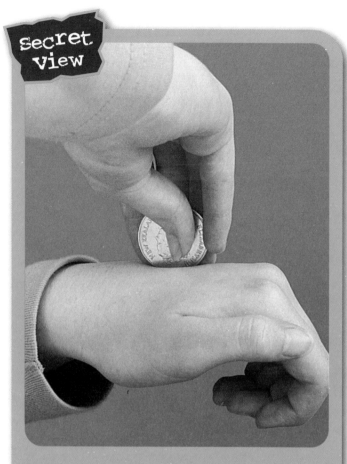

4 Turn your left hand back over. Carry on sliding the coin sideways until it is completely covered by the right hand fingers.

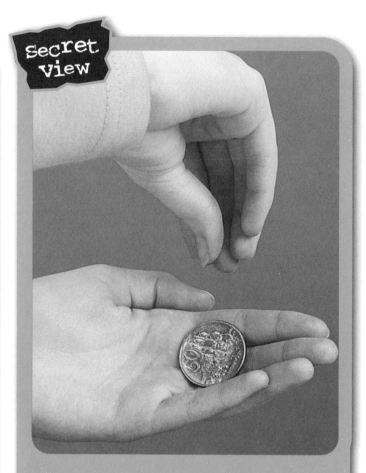

5 Once again, freeze the right hand, while turning the left hand palm up. Point out that the coin is nearly through. As you turn your left palm down once more, drop the coin from your right hand. It is caught by the left hand in the curled fingers just as it completes its turn.

6 Continue to hold the right hand as if it still has the coin. Give the imaginary coin another rub on the back of the hand and slowly open the fingers as you give it a final push.

7 Lift your right hand off and show that the coin has gone. Turn your left hand over to reveal that the coin has penetrated your hand.

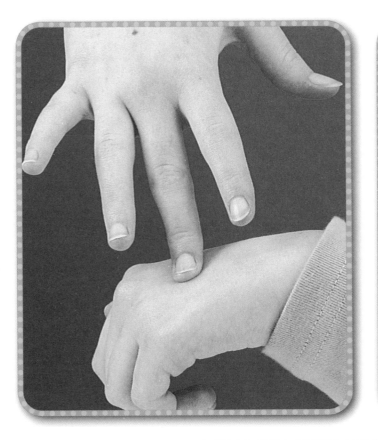

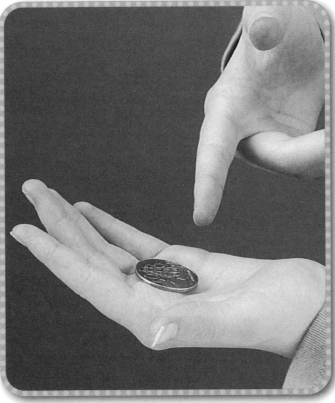

Extra Tips

✱ The secret lies in the timing. You have to synchronize dropping the coin from the right-hand fingers at the exact moment when the left hand is turning over. Try to minimize any finger movement from either hand. The coin just falls onto the left curled fingers—there should be no catching motion.

✱ Before you begin the trick, explain that you have a slot in the back of your hand. Nobody will believe you but insist it is true. Point to the back of your hand explaining where the slot is. You want to give the impression the coin is gradually disappearing down the slot.

Notable Number

In this trick you demonstrate how you have predicted a chosen number in advance. The fact that you might have just struck lucky, with a one in nine chance, makes it even more baffling.

1 You need nine pieces of card cut up into approximately half an inch square and a cup. All of the pieces of card are blank on both sides. On one of them you secretly write the number 5 on the back. This matches a prediction you have already written down on a piece of paper.

2 Begin by laying the pieces of card on the table, making sure the number 5 is not seen. Remember which card it is. Your prediction is folded in half. You are ready to begin.

3 Write the figure 1 on one of the pieces of card. Pick it up, show both sides, and drop it in the cup. Do the same with a second piece of card, writing 2 on it this time. Again show there is nothing on the back.

4 Continue with the third and fourth cards, writing 3 and 4 on them, but this time do not show the blank back when you put them in the cup.

5 When you come to writing 5, make sure you use the same card that you have already written 5 on the back of. Place it in the cup.

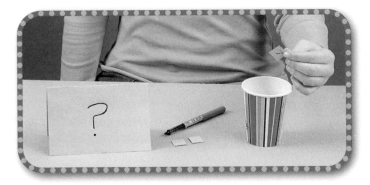

6 Continue with the remaining 4 pieces of cards, writing 6 to 9; again you can show the blank backs on a couple of them when you put them in the cup.

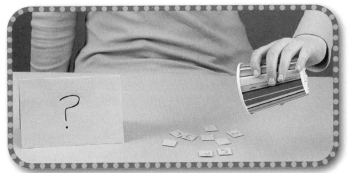

7 Give the cup a thorough shake and then spill the pieces of card out onto the table.

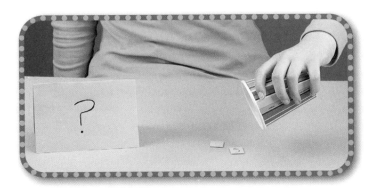

8 Explain any cards that are blank; in other words, if no number shows, you will eliminate them. Pick these up and place them in your pocket. Return the remaining pieces, where a number shows, to the cup.

9 Continue shaking the cards and throwing them on the table until all are eliminated except one. This leaves the card with 5 written on it. Show your prediction is correct.

Extra Tips

✳ Notice the subtle way you show some of the cards blank on both sides as you put them in the cup. Obviously, do not draw attention to this or someone will want to check them all.

Not a Knot

There are many ways of tying a false knot in a handkerchief. This one is especially impressive because the knot gets tighter before it dissolves. It was devised by Joe Berg.

1 Hold a handkerchief at one corner clipped at the edge between your left index and middle fingers. The edge of the handkerchief should not be seen through your fingers. Pick up the adjacent corner with your right hand and bring this corner so it is held, sticking out, by your left thumb and index finger.

2 Grasp the new adjacent corner with the right hand.

3 Tie these two corners together in a normal knot. That is, looking down on the handkerchief, place the left corner on top of the right corner. Bring it down and tuck it through and underneath.

4 While you are doing this make sure the original corner remains clipped in place between the index and middle fingers of your left hand.

5 As you complete the knot, your right hand grasps two strands of the handkerchief. It takes the left corner of the knot between the index and middle fingers while the clipped part of the handkerchief, held by the left hand, is taken between the index finger and thumb.

6 In the meantime, take the right corner of the knot between the index finger and thumb of your left hand.

7 Start to pull the two ends of the handkerchief away from each other, the normal actions for tightening a knot. As you do so, let go of that part of the handkerchief held by the right hand index and middle fingers. This leaves the handkerchief held by the index finger and thumb of each hand.

8 By continuing to pull the two ends apart, the part of the handkerchief you have just let go of recedes into the middle of the knot. Continue pulling; the knot apparently gets smaller and tighter until it suddenly dissolves.

Extra Tips

✴ This will take a little practice to get the knack of it. You need the right tension so that the part of the handkerchief you release—held between the right index and middle finger—gets caught up in the main knot. But not enough to tangle the handkerchief into a genuine knot.

X-Ray Crayons

Pretending you can see without your eyes is a favorite effect of mind readers. You need several colored crayons. They should be exactly the same except for being different colors. You also need a large handkerchief or scarf.

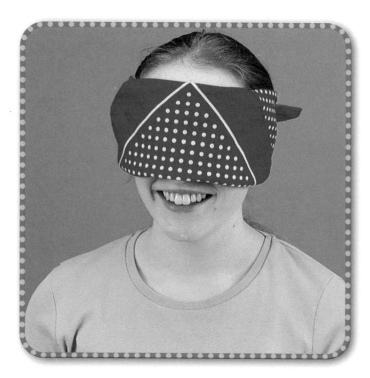

1 The scarf is rolled up and then tied around your head so it covers your eyes.

2 Even though it seems you cannot see, if you look directly down the two sides of your nose you still have limited vision.

3 Place one of your hands behind your back and ask someone to place a crayon in it. You have no idea which it is. Put your other hand behind your back and scrape a bit of the crayon on your fingernail. The audience cannot see this.

Secret View

4 Still holding the crayon behind your back with one hand, bring your other hand to your front.

Extra Tips

✳ This trick is doubly deceptive. Even if some-one suspects you can see through the blindfold, he will still be unable to work out how you see the color of the crayon.

✳ The trick can be instantly repeated with another crayon. Try to vary how you glimpse the color on your nail.

✳ Inform your audience that your fingers are so sensitive that by touch alone you can recognize color.

5 Stroke your chin as if concentrating on which crayon it is. As you are doing this, look down the side of your nose and check the color of the crayon on your nail.

6 After a little more thinking, tell everyone the color of the crayon.

Bank Roller

Any trick involving money is fascinating to people, so you can guarantee attention when you ask to borrow some bills for this intriguing stunt. You need two bills of different denominations.

1 Place one bill on top of the other so they form a V shape. The point of the V is nearest to you and the bill on the top is on your right as you are looking at it.

2 Slightly angle the V shape so that the right-hand bill, is ahead of the left-hand one. Roll up the two bills together.

3 As you complete the rolling up of the left-hand bill, a little corner of the right-hand bill remains exposed. Ask someone to put her finger on this corner and not to take it off.

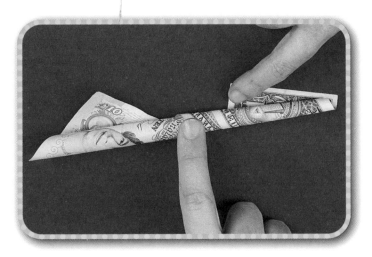

4 Let the top corner of the left-hand bill, which is now completely rolled up, flip over.

Extra Tips

✶ A fun way to present this is as an observation test. Ask someone which bill is on top. As you are rolling up the bills, repeat the question. If the reply is hesitant, unroll the bills and start again.

✶ Explain that you want her finger placed on the corner of the right-hand bill to make sure it remains on top.

✶ This also provides good misdirection for the moment of flipping over the corner of the other bill. Try not to make this too obvious.

✶ Before you begin to unroll the bills, ask again which one is on top. This makes the transfer of the two bills that much more impressive.

5 Put your own finger on this flipped-over corner and carefully unroll the two bills. The bill that was originally on top is now underneath.

Card Prediction

Although a straightforward self-working card trick, this is still puzzling. The more seriously you present it, the more likely you are to convince your audience that you have done something really amazing.

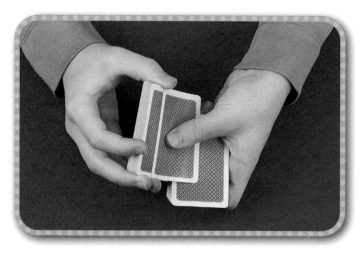

1 Start by having a deck of cards shuffled.

2 Take the cards back and say you are going to make a prediction.

3 Keep the cards facing toward you and note the top two cards. You need to find the card that matches the suit of one of the cards and the value of the other.

4 If, for instance, the king of hearts and seven of spades are the top two cards, you want either the king of spades or the seven of hearts. It does not matter which.

5 Remove that card, say the seven of hearts, without anyone else seeing it. Place it face down on the table. State that this is your prediction card. Give the deck back to your helper. Have someone give you any number between 11 and 20. That number of cards is dealt face down in a pile on the table.

6 Instruct that this pile is to be picked up and then dealt into two more separate piles, alternating between each. Turn the top card of each pile face up. Point out that one card is a seven and the other a heart so together they represent the seven of hearts.

7 Turn your prediction card over.

Extra Tips

✳ This works however many cards are initially dealt on the table; but by limiting the choice of number you give the impression that you are somehow influencing your helper to choose a specific one.

✳ Also, you want at least ten cards dealt; otherwise, the secret of the trick may become obvious. More than twenty cards and it can become a little tedious.

✳ A problem arises if the top two cards are of the same value or the same suit. In that case cut the deck in your hands so you have different cards at the top.

Solid through Solid

A penetration is one of the basic magic effects. That you can do this through your own arm is particularly impressive. You need a 3-foot (91-cm) length of string or rope tied in a continuous loop.

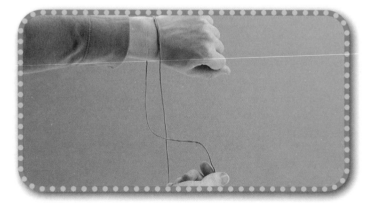

1 Begin by placing the loop over your left wrist.

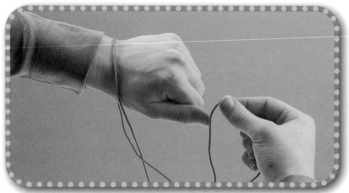

2 Your right hand goes into the loop, palm up, and grips the center of the string furthest away from you between the right thumb and index finger.

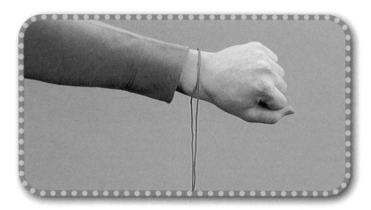

3 Bring the right hand toward you so it crosses the string nearest to you. The string is in the form of a figure eight.

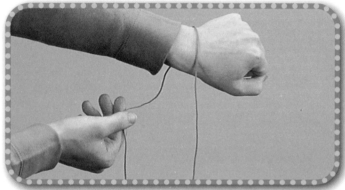

4 Turn your right hand palm downward. This creates a third loop in the string.

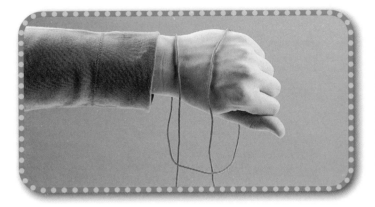

5 Place this loop over your left hand to join the one already on the wrist.

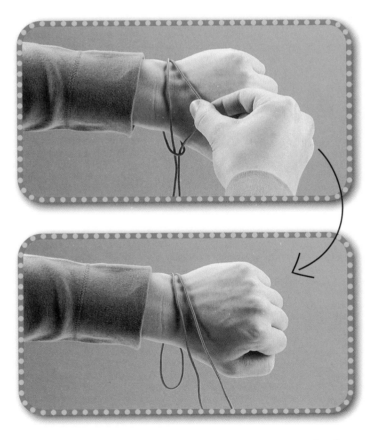

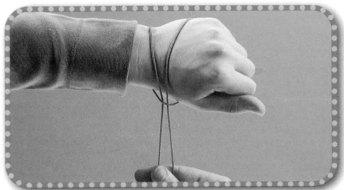

6 Pull down on the center of the bottom loop of the string. The string appears to be securely tied onto your wrist. Tug on it a couple of times to show this.

7 Pull on either of the two strands of string around your wrist and the entire string appears to penetrate through.

Extra Tips

✶ There should be no hesitation in looping the string around your wrist. Stress that you are hooking it around your wrist twice to make sure it is securely tied on.

✶ Keep the knot on the string at the top of your wrist; otherwise it will get caught up when you demonstrate the penetration.

Straw Cutting

Often so-called impromptu magic is not at all; there has been some advance preparation. However if you give the impression that it is impromptu, you create a real impact. This is one such trick.

1 Cut a slit of about 1½ inches (38 mm) lengthwise in the center of a drinking straw. You need a small pair of sharp scissors to do the cutting.

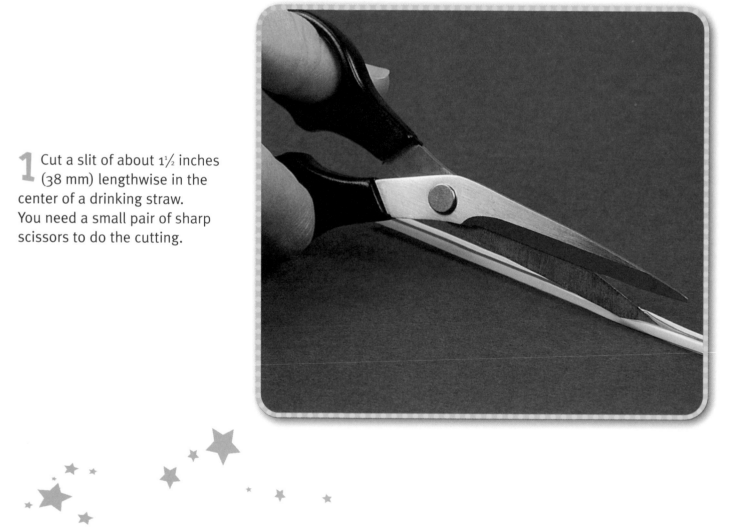

2 Thread a shoelace through the straw so it is hanging the same distance from each end.

3 Bend the straw in half in the middle of the slit. This leaves the straw doubled up with the slit hidden from view.

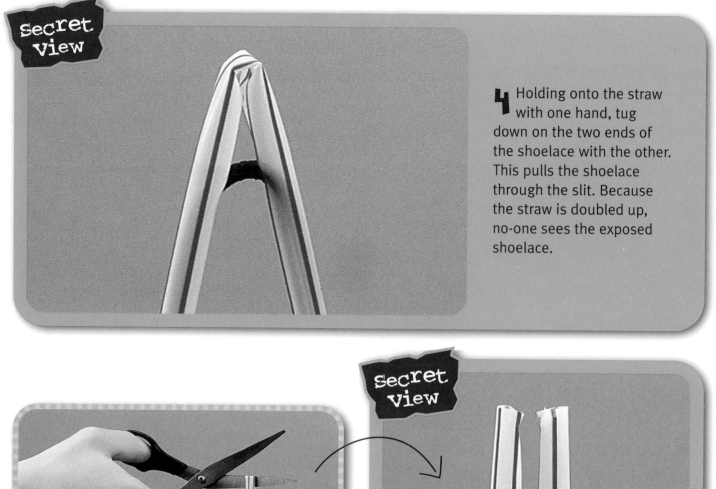

4 Holding onto the straw with one hand, tug down on the two ends of the shoelace with the other. This pulls the shoelace through the slit. Because the straw is doubled up, no-one sees the exposed shoelace.

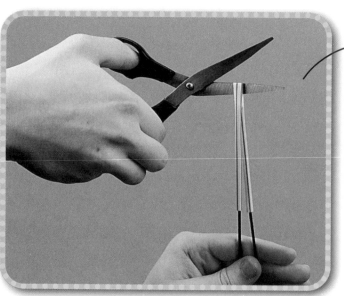

Secret View

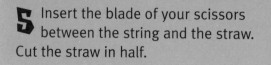

5 Insert the blade of your scissors between the string and the straw. Cut the straw in half.

6 Placing your fingers over the two cut pieces of straw, straighten them up. Pull them apart to reveal that the shoelace remains uncut.

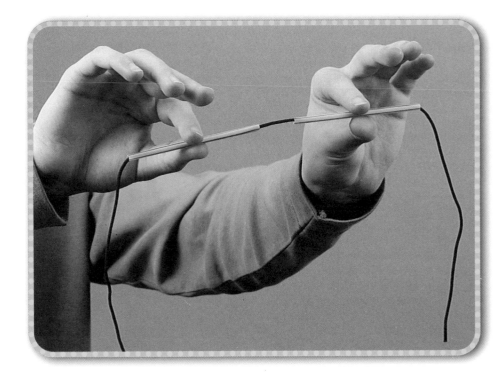

Extra Tips

✻ To make this trick appear entirely impromptu, place your prepared straw among some others. To recognize which it is, put a slight crease near the top by bending it.

✻ Using someone's shoelace makes the trick seem spontaneous. It is also amusing as the lender will be most concerned about the fate of his shoelace.

✻ When you cut through the straw, make it appear quite hard—remember, you are supposed to be cutting through a shoelace as well.

✻ At the end, squash up the two bits of straw and toss them aside. Nobody should want to look at them; they will be too busy checking the shoelace.

Balloon Burst

Here you have a great mini-illusion with very few props. You need a balloon, some transparent sticky tape, and a long pin or needle; the latter should be as sharp as possible.

1 In preparation, blow up the balloon and tie a knot in the end. Take a piece of the transparent sticky tape about 2 inches (5 cm) in length. Stick this on the balloon.

2 To perform the trick, pick up your long pin and prepare to push it through the middle of the tape on the balloon.

3 Slowly push the pin into the balloon. It will not burst.

4 Remove the pin. Finish by bursting the balloon by pricking it somewhere else on its surface.

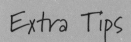

Extra Tips

✳ It might be best to have a couple of balloons spare in case one accidentally bursts during performance. If this happens, do not worry. It will look even more impressive when you succeed.

✳ If you have two pieces of tape at either end of the balloon, you can push the pin all the way through.

Bow and Arrow

One of the clichés in magic is that the hand is quicker than the eye. This is not true. Nevertheless, with this trick you give the impression you move so fast nobody can detect what is happening. It can be performed with a piece of rope or a handkerchief. It is explained here with string.

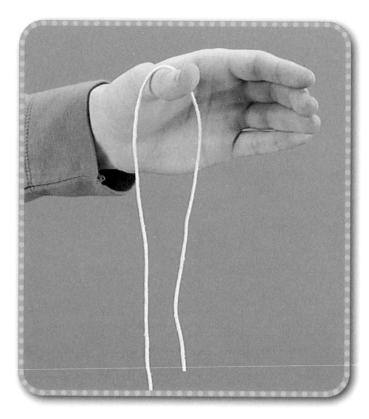

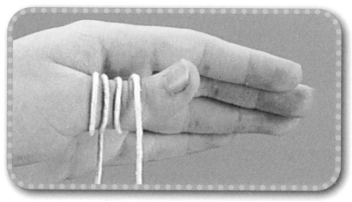

2 Start wrapping the longer end of the string quite tightly around your thumb about three or four times.

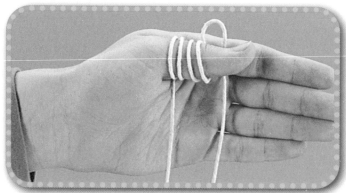

1 You need a piece of string about 2 feet (5 cm) long. Place the string between the thumb and finger of your left hand in the crotch of your thumb. The palm of your hand is facing you, your thumb on top. About two-thirds of the string is hanging in front of your thumb as you are looking at your hand; about one-third is behind.

3 Make a small loop by bringing the string up behind your thumb.

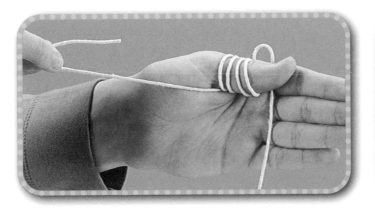

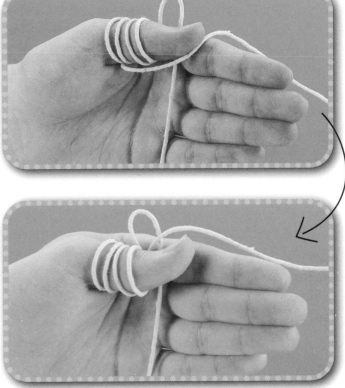

4 Take hold of the original shorter end of the string with your right hand and pull it toward yourself. Line it up with the loop, making a number of short, practice jabs.

Extra Tips

✶ **Explain to the audience in advance what you are going to do. Tell them you are going to thread one end of the string through the loop so fast they will not be able to see it. You are challenging them to detect you. This is seldom recommended in magic but in this trick you can get away with it.**

5 Move your hand forward as if aiming to put the end through the loop. However, pass just to the right of the loop, dragging the string between your left thumb and index finger. You do not have to open them up; the forceful jerk will squeeze the string between them. Make sure the end is pulled tight at the finish. It appears that the string is threaded through the loop.

Frustrating Pencil

Here is a way of really annoying your friends. It is both puzzling and immensely irritating! You will need an unsharpened pencil and a short piece of string.

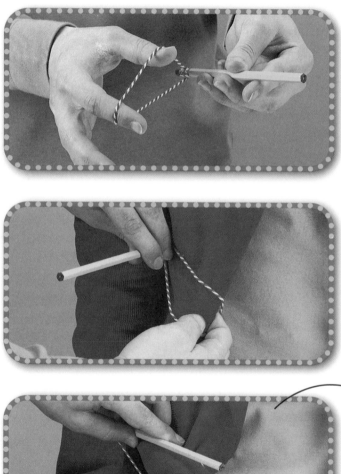

1 Cut a groove all around near the end of the pencil and tie a loop of string around it. The loop is slightly shorter than the pencil so the pencil cannot swing through it. Hold the loop of string open with your right index finger and thumb.

2 Look for a suitable victim and grasp his shirt or jacket next to a buttonhole with the same finger and thumb. Pull the material through the loop. Your left hand holds the end of the pencil with the attached string.

3 Stretch out the loop until it is far out enough for the other end of the pencil to go through the buttonhole.

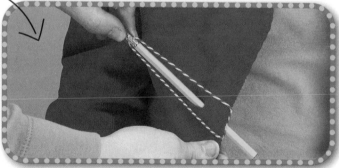

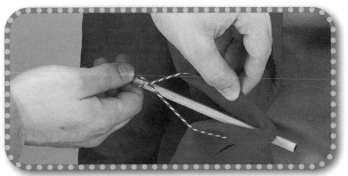

4 Once it is through, pull the pencil tight so it is knotted to the buttonhole.

5 Challenge him to get the pencil off the buttonhole without cutting the string.

7 Grasping the cloth next to the buttonhole, pull the pencil back through the loop.

6 To release him, begin by loosening the knot. Then push the string end of the pencil through the buttonhole from the inside of the shirt or jacket.

8 When there is sufficient slack push the end of the pencil completely free of the buttonhole.

Extra Tips

✶ Experiment first with your own buttonhole before trying it on someone else. After a little practice you can almost instantly loop the pencil onto someone's jacket.

Disappearing Coin

Although quite simple this trick has a big impact. It was a feature trick for the famous magician Max Malini. Along with a coin, you need a piece of paper about 4 x 6 inches (10 x 15 cm). It should not be too thick as you are going to have to tear it up when folded.

1 Place the coin in the middle of the folded sheet. Begin by folding the sheet in half so that one side of the paper is about an inch (2.5 cm) shorter than the other.

2 You are now going to fold the sheet into three. This is done by doubling back the sides, away from you and toward your audience. Do this slowly and carefully.

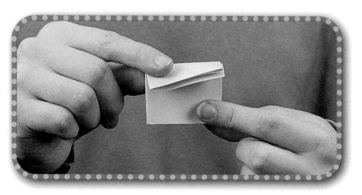

3 Then fold the top of the bundle down and away from you. This seems to be sealing the coin inside. However, because of the first out-of-place fold, there is now a gap in top of the bundle.

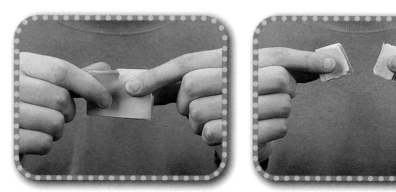

4 Take the bundle by the right hand at the top, your fingers making sure the coin does not come out unexpectedly. Have a spectator verify that the coin is still there. Alternatively, tap it on a glass or other solid object.

6 Tear the bundle in half. Put the two halves together and tear into quarters. The coin has vanished.

Secret View

5 Turn the bundle upward and release the thumb's grip. In the process let the coin slip out of the bundle and fall into the right hand so that it rests at the bottom of your fingers.

Extra Tips

* Once you have torn up the pieces, as far as the audience is concerned the trick is now over. Do not be in too much of a hurry to get rid of the coin. Relax with it hidden in your hand. After a short period get rid of the coin by placing it, along with the torn paper, in your pocket or a bag.

* Try to use as large a coin as possible. The heavier it is, the easier it will slip from the piece of paper into your hand.

Glass through Table

If you want to really amaze your audience, then this is the trick for you. Sit at a table so your knees are together and comfortably tucked underneath. You also need a glass, a coin, and a sheet of newspaper.

1 Wrap the glass in the paper so its edge aligns with the rim of the glass. Twist it at the base so the paper will not unravel.

2 Cover the coin with the inverted glass and ask someone to guess whether it is showing heads or tails.

3 To reveal the answer, lift up the glass and hold it so that its rim is just below the top of the table.

4 Turn the coin over a few times and place the glass on top of it once more. Again ask whether she thinks it is showing heads or tails.

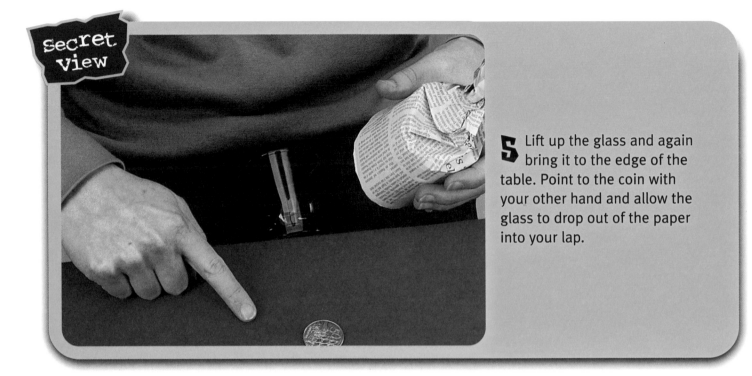

5 Lift up the glass and again bring it to the edge of the table. Point to the coin with your other hand and allow the glass to drop out of the paper into your lap.

6 Bring the paper shell back over the table on top of the coin. Put both your hands on top of the paper and press down suddenly, squashing the paper shell flat.

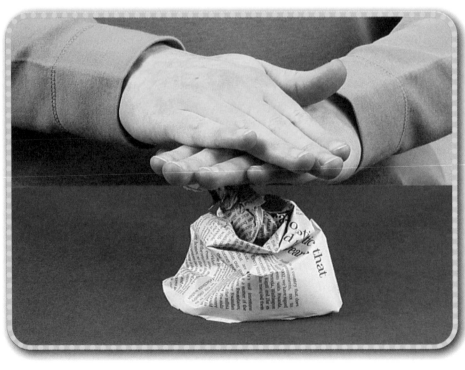

✳ The misdirection for this trick comes from the very start. Your supposed reason for wrapping up the glass in the paper is so nobody can see whether the coin is showing heads or tails. Your full attention is always on the coin; for the audience the glass is not important until the unexpected end.

✳ Wrapping up the glass in the paper requires some practice. When you firmly grasp the paper, you lift up both the paper and the glass together. If you relax your grip, the glass slips out of the paper. In doing this, however, the shape of the paper is retained.

✳ Make sure your audience cannot see your lap. If you lean forward when dropping the glass, this helps to hide it.

✳ It is best if everyone is sitting in front of you.

7 Reach under the table and bring the glass back out from your lap. The glass seems to have penetrated through the table.

8 Do not worry about the coin; everyone will be so amazed they will have no interest in that anymore.

Endless Chain

There are many tricks that started out as a means of fleecing the unwary; but have been adapted by magicians for entertainment purposes. This is one such trick.

1 Ideally you need a loop of thin chain around 3 feet in length. Soft string is a reasonable substitute but not as good.

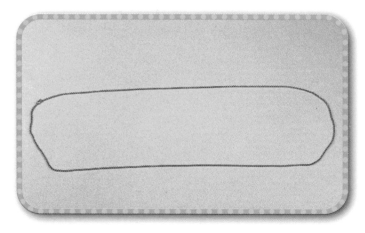

2 Place the chain on the table in a long loop.

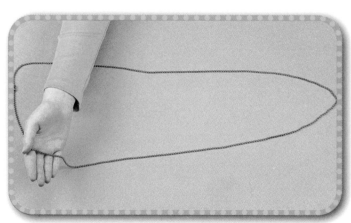

3 With your left hand pick up the chain at the outer right-hand side and place it on top of your palm-up right hand. The right-hand fingers are underneath, the thumb on top.

4 Turn your right hand over, dragging the chain with it, forming a C shape.

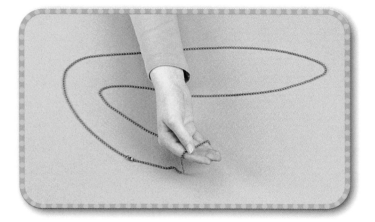

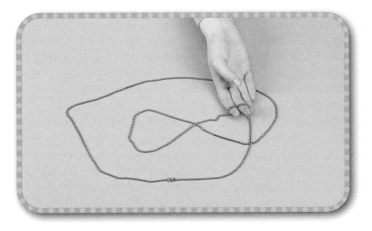

5 Bring the loop you are holding over the top of the left-hand side of the outer chain and place it on the table. It looks like a figure eight inside an outer circle.

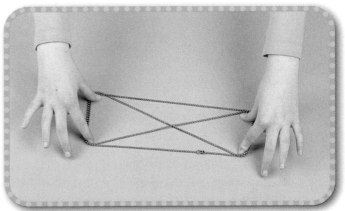

6 Place the first finger and thumb of each hand in either side of the loop of the figure eight and straighten them. This results in a rectangle with two diagonals.

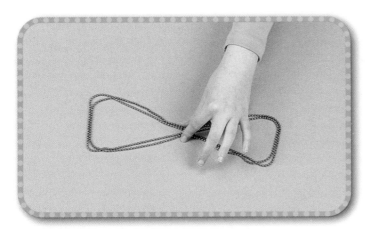

7 Finally squeeze the two centers of the rectangle inward to form another figure eight.

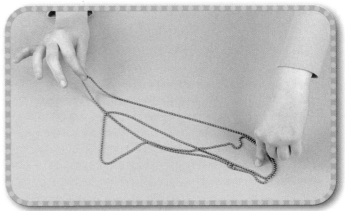

8 If a finger is placed in the left-hand side of the figure eight, and either end of the right-hand chain pulled away, the finger is trapped.

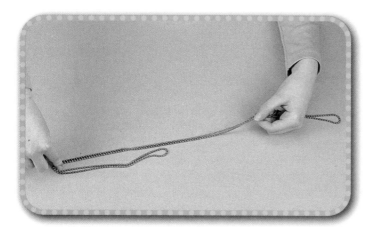

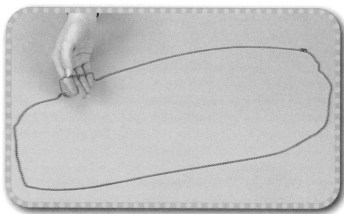

9 If the finger is placed in the right-hand side of the figure eight, and either end of the left-hand chain pulled away, the chain comes away.

10 The challenge is for the spectator to guess which side of the chain he has to put his finger in so it is trapped. If the chain comes free, he loses.

11 When demonstrating how he can win or lose, lay out the chain as just described.

12 However when you get him to play, the chain is laid out slightly differently. Instead of picking up the strand of the chain furthest away from you, pick up the part nearest to you.

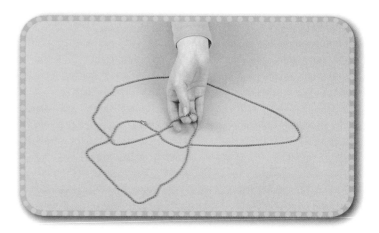

13 This time bring your right hand over the outer chain on the loop, forming a figure eight.

14 Continue round and place it down on the table. This looks like a figure eight in the middle of two loops.

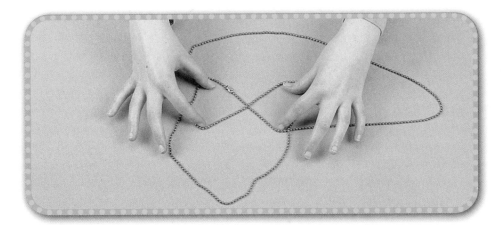

15 Repeat the actions of creating the rectangle with diagonals and the final figure eight.

16 Whichever side of the chain your helper puts his finger in, the chain slips free.

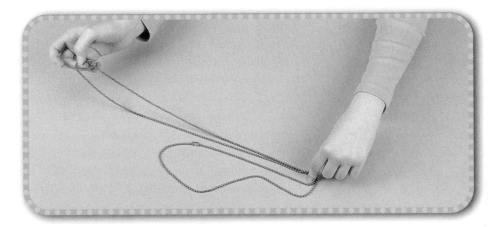

Extra Tips

✶ Practice making both figures smoothly so they look identical when laying them out.

✶ A good finish is to get your helper to place a finger in both sides of the figure eight. Pull the chain and they are both trapped. Ask him to lift up either finger and the chain comes free!

Sleight of hand means a deceptive technique with the hands, frequently involving ordinary objects such as cards, coins, and billiard balls. The most common sleights involve vanishing, appearing, or changing the props in some way. Many of the tricks in this book do not require any such secret manipulation; magicians call these self-working tricks, so it is possible to do some excellent magic without learning sleight of hand.

To become proficient at magic, however, it is important to learn some sleights. Many of the best tricks, or classic tricks as they are often referred to, require some degree of sleight of hand. Also, besides expanding your repertoire, sleight of hand assists in improving your self-working tricks. Here are some of the reasons:

● It helps you handle all your props in an elegant way. People are more entertained if tricks are performed with style and grace.

● Learning sleight of hand teaches you how to practice. And even the easiest trick, if you want to do it well, requires some practice.

● If you perform some sleight of hand, your audience will assume all your tricks are done like that. So when you perform a self-working trick, the audience is less likely to work out the solution.

● It allows you to improvise your way out of trouble. Should something unfortunately go wrong with the trick, some sleight of hand might help you recover the situation.

Learning sleights requires practice; and this sounds like hard work. But practicing should be fun. Indeed, it has to be enjoyable for you to want to do it. It is pointless trying to force someone to practice a new skill. He will just end up doing it badly, which is worse than not learning it at all.

Here are some guidelines in practicing:

● Initially read all the instructions. Make sure you understand exactly what you are aiming for.

● Then go through one step at a time. Master the first step before moving onto the next.

● It is best if you divide up your practicing into small chunks. Practice for about ten minutes and then take a break.

● Concentrate on one sleight or trick at a time. That is better than practicing lots of different ones and ending up doing all of them rather poorly.

The best sleight of hand to start off with involves playing cards and coins. Once you have learned just a few sleights, there are dozens of different tricks you can perform with them. Indeed, there are some magicians who earn their living performing with only a deck of cards and a few coins.

The card section teaches you how to keep control of a card and how to make sure a specific card is selected.

The coin section teaches you how to conceal a coin in your hand, how to make a coin disappear, and how to change one coin for another.

Some tricks using these sleights are also taught.

Above ➤ Sleight-of-hand expert, Edouard Brunnet, asks "Is this your card?"

CARD SLEIGHTS

How to Control a Card

A lot of card tricks depend on keeping track of a card in the deck; this is known as controlling a card. For instance, if you know a chosen card is at the top of the deck, but your audience thinks it is lost somewhere in the deck, there are many tricks you can now do.

Controlling a card can be broken down into three steps. First, have a card selected from the deck; second have it returned, and finally, convince your audience that it is lost in the deck.

The Overhand Shuffle

The first thing you have to learn is how to shuffle a deck of cards. You may already be familiar with the method below. Nevertheless, it is vital that you learn it exactly as written if you want to subsequently properly control a card.

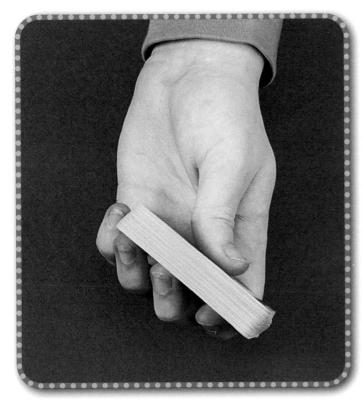

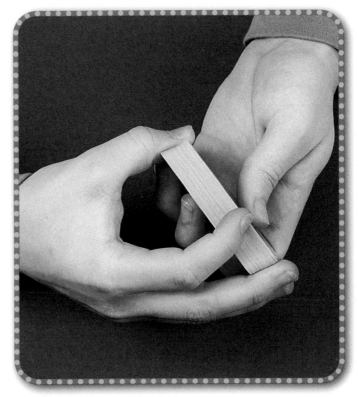

1 Hold the deck vertically in your left hand with your thumb against the top card and your other fingers supporting the bottom card. Your little finger rests at the inner end of the deck.

2 Your right hand comes down on top of the cards, the thumb at the inner end, first finger on top, and the other fingers at the outer end.

3 Your right hand lifts up about three-quarters of the bottom part of the deck. To assist in this task, the left thumb reaches to the top of the deck and grips the remaining quarter.

5 The left thumb reaches up and grips one or two cards at the top and front. The right hand lifts the rest of the cards straight up, leaving the gripped cards to fall on top of those already held in your left hand.

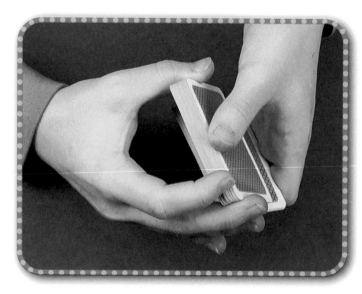

4 The portion of the deck held in the right hand lifts up and over, and then comes down in front of, the remaining quarter.

6 The above step is then repeated. That is, the right hand comes back down again in front of the cards in the left hand. The left thumb pulls off a few more cards as the right hand lifts the rest of the deck up again.

7 By continuously doing this, all the cards in the right hand are gradually pulled off on top of the cards held in the left hand.

8 When there are only a few more cards left in the right hand, drop them on top of those in the left hand. The shuffle is then complete.

9 Practice pulling off just one card with your left thumb as well as chunks of cards. To do this, your left thumb rests on the back of the top card, rather than gripping the top edge. The thumb drags the card down as your right hand lifts the remaining cards upward.

Extra Tips

✳ Try not to look at the deck when you shuffle the cards.

✳ Keeping your left little finger resting at the end of the deck will probably seem unnatural at first, but it assists in keeping the cards neatly squared as you carry out your shuffle. It is also essential later on for assisting in controlling the card.

Selection of the Card

Pick up the deck of cards and perform the overhand shuffle. This convinces everyone that you have absolutely no idea where any specific cards may be in the deck.

1 Hold the cards face down in the palm of your left hand, your thumb lying along one side, your fingers along the other.

2 With your left thumb start to push cards off the top of the deck. As you do so the other cards below them begin to spread to your right.

3 Bring your right hand toward the cards.

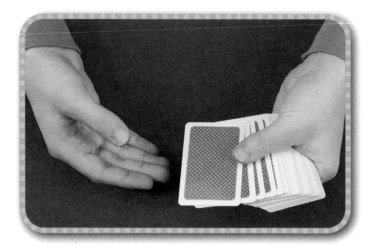

4 Your right hand comes over, mirroring the position of your left hand, and takes the pushed-off cards.

5 After you have pushed off some more cards into your right hand, both hands can spread apart a little. The cards in the middle of the deck are balanced, one on top of each other, between your two hands.

6 In this position offer the cards for somebody to select one.

7 As soon as the card is removed, push your two hands together to even up the cards.

8 If you like you can go straight into another overhand shuffle.

Extra Tips

✱ Spreading the cards like this reassures everyone that the choice of card is absolutely fair.

✱ By shuffling the cards both before and after the selection, you are getting your audience used to the control that is about to take place.

Return of the Card

Before having a selected card returned to the deck, make sure everybody has looked at the card. You do not want to come to the finish of the trick and nobody can remember what it is!

1 Hold the deck as if about to begin an overhand shuffle. Lift off the back three quarters, again as if about to start a shuffle. Move your left hand forward with the remaining quarter of the deck toward the person who holds the selected card.

2 The cards rest on your fingers with the left little finger at the far end. Ask for the card to be replaced on top.

3 If necessary, with your left thumb maneuver the returned card so it is even with the other cards.

Control of the Card

At the end of this sequence the selected card should be at the top of the deck. However, the audience should be convinced the card is lost somewhere in the middle of the deck.

1 You are now going straight into an overhand shuffle. However, rather than dropping two or three cards, just drag off the top card with your thumb.

2 This card is back down from the other cards in the left hand, so it sticks out from the rear. This is known as an "injog." Notice how the card rests on the tip of your left little finger.

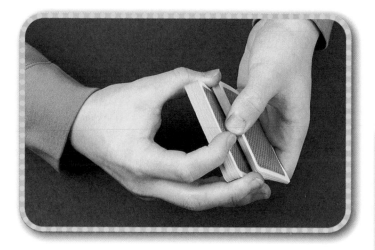

3 Continue shuffling the rest of the cards on top of those in the left hand in the normal way.

4 At the finish the audience should be totally unaware of the injogged card; it is covered by the other cards shuffled on top.

5 The selected card is directly underneath the injogged card. You need to bring that card to the top of the deck.

6 Bring your right hand forward to start another overhand shuffle. This time though your thumb at the inner end pushes against the injogged card. This opens up a gap above the selected card at the near end of the deck.

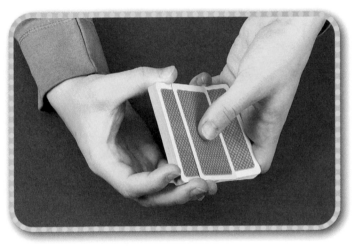

7 The right hand holds the deck with the index finger on top, the other fingers at the outer end, and the thumb keeping separate the two portions of the deck at the inner end. Looking down from above, the deck is in a V shape.

8 Proceed from here straight into your shuffle. The left thumb removes a few cards from the top of the deck while the right hand lifts up the rest of the deck. Your right thumb retains the break between the two portions.

9 Continue pulling off cards from the right hand as usual until you have shuffled off all the cards above the break.

Extra Tips

✱ As you start to practice, leave the injogged card a long way out from the back of the deck. As you get better, it needs to stick out only a little.

✱ If you can, try to avoid looking at the deck as you do the control.

10 Finish by dropping the remaining cards in your right hand on top of those in your left.

11 The selected card is now on top of the deck.

How to Force a Card

When spectators think they have a free choice of card, but the magician knows what it is, this is called forcing a card. This means the card can be returned to the deck and genuinely shuffled.

3 If you like, perform the injog control to retain the remembered card at the top.

1 To force a card you need to know the top card of the deck. Here is a subtle way of observing it: Begin in the starting position of the overhand shuffle. Push your left fingers forward against the bottom card tilting the deck. By looking down you can see the card.

2 Begin an overhand shuffle. When you have almost completed the shuffle, draw single cards off with your left thumb. The very last card that you shuffle on top is your remembered bottom card.

4 Place the deck on the table and ask someone to cut the deck in half. It does not matter where it is cut so long as you remember which is the top half.

5 Pick up the bottom half and place it at right angles on top of the top half. Explain to the audience you are marking where the deck was cut.

6 After a short time, lift off the top half and ask somebody to look at the top card of the pile underneath. Of course, the card is the same one you recall. This is known as the crisscross force.

Extra Tips

✳ This may seem very bold but it works. People do not remember which is the original top half of the deck. Also, by fairly shuffling the deck first nobody is aware you are familiar with any of the cards.

✳ Try to leave a little time between making the crisscross cut and allowing your helper to check the card.

✳ The subtle look at the card at the bottom of the deck before the shuffle is called a glimpse.

SLEIGHT-OF-HAND CARD TRICKS

WHILE YOU CAN CONTINUALLY USE THE OVERHAND SHUFFLE CONTROL, BE WARY OF USING THE CRISSCROSS FORCE MORE THAN ONCE TO THE SAME AUDIENCE. THE FIRST TWO TRICKS USE THE OVERHAND SHUFFLE AND THE THIRD ONE THE CRISSCROSS FORCE.

Tracker Card

There are many different ways of finding a selected card once it is controlled to the top of the deck. In this trick another card is used to magically track down the selected card.

1 Have one person select a card and return it to the deck. Control it to the top with the overhand shuffle. Assume it is the ten of diamonds.

2 Spread the cards again for another card to be chosen. This time, though, just ask for a card to be touched rather then removed. Assume it is the jack of spades. Although neither you nor your helper know this yet.

3 Break the deck in half at that point. Keep the touched card on top of the left-hand half and push the card slightly to the right with your thumb.

4 Turn the cards in your right hand face up by turning your right palm down.

5 Place these cards on top of the selected card, clipping the touched card with your thumb.

6 Turn the hand palm up again retaining the touched card with the thumb. The deck of cards is face down with the touched card face up.

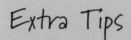

Extra Tips

✷ Practice the turning over of the touched card so it is done smoothly. You are doing it very openly. As far as the audience is aware, the reason for the move is only to turn the card face up.

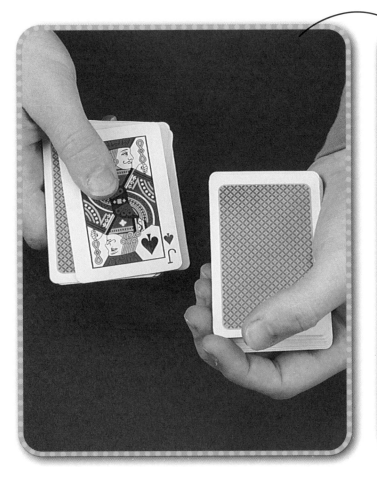

7 Place the cards in the left hand on top of the face-up card. Then even up the cards.

8 By these actions the touched card is now directly above the original selected card. Explain that the touched card is going to try and track down the chosen card in the deck. Spread the cards, turn over the card underneath the jack of spades, and show you have succeeded.

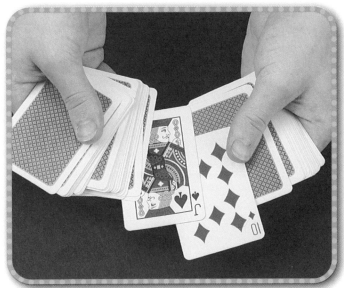

Jumping Card

If your audience are convinced the selected card is completely lost in the deck, this trick is extremely impressive. The card seems to the audience to appear from nowhere.

1 Have a card selected and controlled to the top with the overhand shuffle. Shuffle the deck a few more times, keeping the card at the top.

2 Hold the deck in your left hand as if you are about to spread the cards. The right hand rests on top of the deck, the fingers in front, thumb behind.

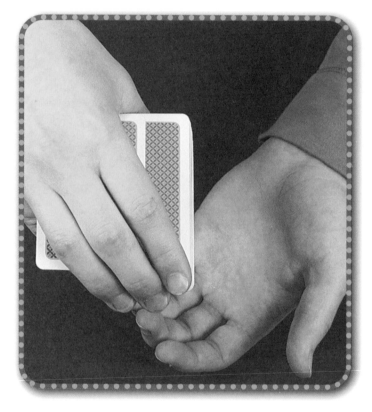

Extra Tips

✴ If done correctly, this should appear as if you have picked up the deck, tossed it down again, and the chosen card jumps out face up.

✴ The pushing over of the top card and the lifting up of the deck are done in the same actions.

3 The left thumb pushes the top card to the right between the third and little finger of the right hand. It is aligned with the deck but halfway over.

4 Gripping the whole deck in the right hand, lift the cards off the left.

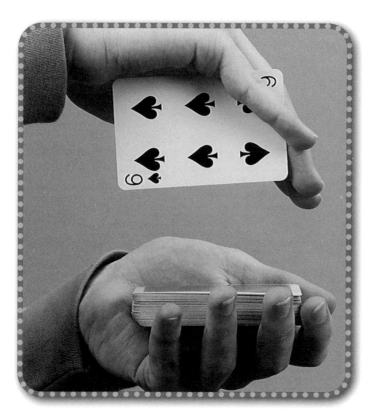

5 Drop the deck back into the left hand. As you do so, the right hand moves upward retaining the selected card between the fingers. Do this with a slight jerk so the card starts to flip over face up.

6 Release the card from your right-hand fingers. The selected card falls face up on top of the rest of the deck in your left hand.

Name Spelling

For this trick you need to know your helper's first name. Assume you know it is John. If you can discover it secretly the trick will be even more impressive.

1 Using the crisscross force, have a known card removed. Say it is the three of diamonds. When the card has been looked at and remembered, have it returned it to the deck. Have the deck shuffled.

2 Take back the deck and start looking through it. The cards are held as if you are about to have a card selected; but face up. Keep the cards toward you so nobody else can see them.

3 Push off cards with your left hand thumb into your right hand until you spot the three of diamonds you forced. Placing your thumb on that card, say the letter J to yourself.

4 Push over the next card with your thumb, calling it O; followed by the next two cards, H and N.

5 Separate your hands. Your right hand holds the half of the deck with the forced card and the three cards above it. Your left hand holds the rest of the deck.

Extra Tips

✶ When looking through the cards, do not try to hide the fact you are trying to find the selected card. Pretend, however, you are having no luck.

✶ If you find the forced card very near the top of the deck, cut the deck in half so it ends up somewhere in the middle. And then start your silent spelling.

✶ Before getting your helper to spell his name, you may want to give the deck an overhand shuffle retaining the four cards on the top.

6 Place the cards in your left hand underneath the cards in your right. This leaves the three of diamonds fourth from the top of the deck.

7 Turn the whole deck face down and square up the cards.

8 Get John to spell out his name, dealing one card for each letter. Turn the final card over to reveal his selection.

COIN SLEIGHTS

MOST PEOPLE CARRY MONEY AROUND WITH THEM, SO IF YOU MASTER THESE COIN SLEIGHTS YOU CAN DO AN INSTANT MAGIC SHOW ANYWHERE AND AT ANY TIME. CHILDREN IN PARTICULAR LOVE SEEING MONEY PRODUCED FROM NOWHERE.

How to Conceal a Coin

The basis of most coin tricks depend on secretly hiding a coin in your hand. It is not hard to keep the coin hidden. The difficult part is making sure your hand looks natural when you do so.

Thumb Palm

1 The coin is clipped at the base of your thumb and held in place.

2 Practice keeping your thumb straight. If it is bent inward the hand appears unnatural.

3 To get the coin into the thumb palm, begin with the coin held at your fingertips between your first two fingers and thumb.

4 Releasing your thumb, curl your fingers inward, pressing the coin into the thumb palm.

Finger Palm

1 The coin rests at the base of the second and third fingers. By slightly curving them inward the coin stays in position.

Extra Tips

✳ Practice shifting the coin from the thumb palm to the finger palm. With the coin held in thumb palm position, bend the second and third fingers inward.

✳ The thumb automatically releases the coin in this action and the coin flips over to end up in finger palm position.

✳ Reverse the procedure to get the coin back into the thumb palm again.

Make a Coin Disappear

There are many ways of vanishing a coin. This method is probably the oldest and still one of the best. Refer to the section on Misdirection (page 13) when going through this.

1 Hold a coin in your right hand between your thumb and index finger. The coin should face the audience.

2 The left hand comes across as if it is about to pick up the coin. The thumb goes behind the coin, the fingers in front.

secret View

3 As the left-hand fingers and thumb pinch together as if to take the coin, let it drop by letting go with your right thumb.

hidden coin

4 The coin lands on your right-hand fingers in finger palm position.

5 The left hand moves away as if it is holding the coin. Focus your attention on your left hand by looking at it.

6 Allow your right hand to drop to your side.

7 After a short time, open your left-hand fingers to show the coin has vanished.

Extra Tips

✷ This trick is called The French Drop. You might even have seen someone try it. It is often done as a challenge—guess which hand the coin is in? This, though, is not really magical.

✷ The hardest part is keeping your right-hand fingers and thumb still when you pretend to take the coin in the left hand. Any sudden movement gives the game away and your audience will no longer be convinced by your "magic."

✷ If you have your angles right, the coin is not seen when it drops on your right-hand fingers. Because there is a gap between your fingers and thumb where the coin used to be, people automatically assume it is in your other hand.

✷ Do not let your right hand fall down to your side until your attention is fully focused on your left hand.

✷ Practice doing The French Drop, reversing the hands.

Make a Coin Appear

Having made a coin disappear, you need to reproduce it at some stage. This is best done from either about your person or from somebody else. Here are a couple of fun reproductions.

1 One of the easiest methods is to find the coin behind your knee. Your hand, with the coin in finger palm position, goes behind your knee.

2 Hidden from view, the thumb pushes the coin forward toward your fingertips.

Extra Tips

✳ Do not be in too much of a hurry to reproduce a coin once you have made it disappear. The audience needs to be convinced first that it has really disappeared.

✳ Pretend to find the coin in other items of clothing such as underneath a tie or in a pocket.

3 Bring the coin out, held by your thumb and fingers close to the edge. You want as much of the coin exposed as possible.

4 It is also very effective to find the coin in someone's clothing. Again, assume you have just done The French Drop and the coin is finger palmed in your right hand.

5 Point your right index finger at someone's jacket. The hand is turned palm down with the other fingers curled inward. In this position the coin is completely hidden from view.

7 Reach under the jacket and remove the coin from your right hand. Keep your right hand still.

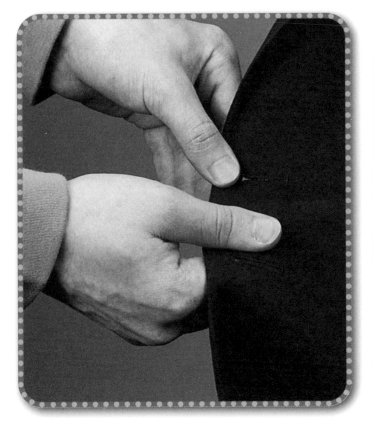

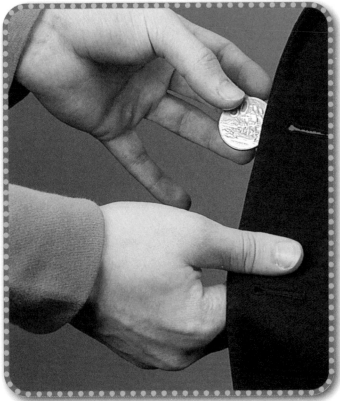

6 With your right hand take the bottom of the jacket and pull it toward you. Your left hand comes in to assist, thumb on top, fingers and coin underneath the jacket.

8 Move your left hand away from the right underneath the jacket. Then slowly pull the coin out at your fingertips.

Change One Coin for Another

Apart from making coins vanish and reappear, the most effective sleight is magically changing one coin for another. This is particularly popular if you change a low value coin for a higher!

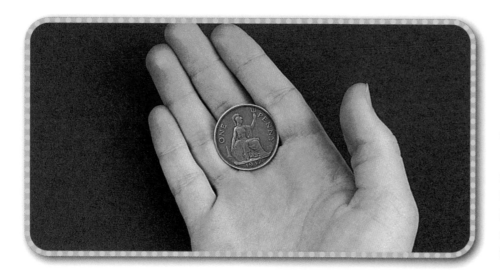

1 You need two different coins. One of the coins is held clipped in your right hand between your first and third fingers at their base.

2 The coin in your right hand is in virtually the same position as the finger palm, except rather than resting on the fingers, it is held. This enables you to stretch out your fingers while retaining the coin.

3 Hold the second coin in your left hand as if you are about to perform The French Drop.

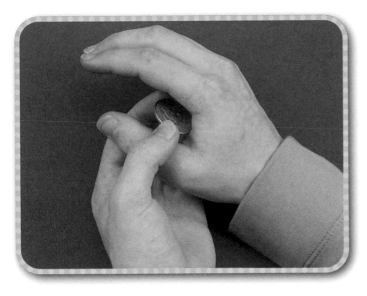

4 Your right-hand fingers move in front of the coin in the left hand; do not let go of it. Keep moving your right hand further across until the left-hand coin goes into the right-hand thumb palm.

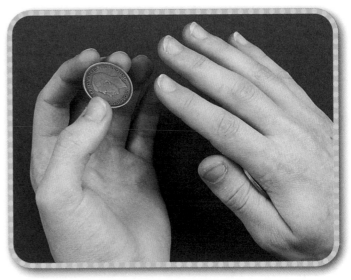

5 As your right hand pulls back, your left-hand finger and thumb pick up the coin previously held by the right hand.

6 As the coin comes into view, spread your right hand fingers wide apart. This helps give the illusion of an instant change of coins.

Extra Tips

✶ Try to minimize the movement of your fingers and thumb, particularly of your left hand. The impression you want to give is of your hand just passing in front of the coin and changing it.

✶ You can repeat the change again by shifting the coin now in the thumb palm back into the finger clip position. This is basically the same movement as you would use to shift it into the finger palm.

Copper Silver Coin Trick

Here is a great coin trick that uses many of the sleights you have learned. You need two coins that are the same and one of a different contrasting color. All the coins should be of similar size. Magicians often use an American half-dollar (silver in color) and an old English penny (copper).

1 Assume you have two silver coins and one copper. Start with all three coins in your pocket.

2 Bring out the copper coin at your fingertips with the silver coin finger palmed in the same hand.

Secret View

Secret View

3 Ask someone to hold out their hand, palm up. Tell her you are going to give her the coin to hold. As your hand comes over to place the coin into her hand, thumb palm the copper coin.

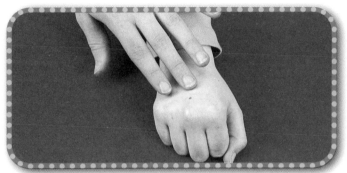

4 Your hand turns face down and places the finger-palmed silver coin in her hand. Keep your hand over the top of her hand so she cannot see the change in coin. Use your other hand to firmly close her fingers.

5 Turn her wrist over, stressing that she must not let go of the coin.

6 Reach into your pocket and take out the second silver coin. As you do so, shift the copper coin from the thumb palm into the finger clip position so that it's ready for the coin change.

7 Holding the silver coin in the other hand, perform the coin change.

Extra Tips

✱ You can place the copper coin back into your pocket without anybody noticing. All attention will be on your helper's amazement.

✱ The reason for turning her wrist upside down is to prevent her from opening her hand prematurely.

✱ Nobody will suspect the presence of a third coin. The coins are of similar size—she will not notice you putting a different coin in her hand.

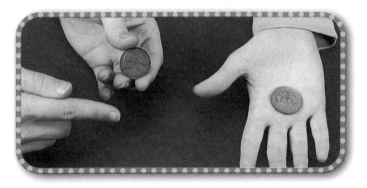

8 Ask your helper to open her hand. She finds she now holds the copper coin.

Conclusion

Remember, the more you practice, the better you will become and the easier you will find it to learn new sleights. If you want to pursue sleight of hand further, here are three books to study:

Jean Hugard and Frederick Braue, *The Royal Road to Card Magic* (New York: Dover Publications, 1999)

J.B. Bobo, *The New Modern Coin Magic* (Chicago: Magic Inc., 1966)

Henry Hay, *The Amateur Magician's Handbook* (Book Sales, 1996)

Index

A

Alan, Don 16
Allerton, Bert 16
*Amateur Magician's Handbook,
 The* (Hay) 189
Anderson, John Henry 55
animals, performing with 26, 53
Annemann, Ted 50
appearance
    comedy magic 18
    mind magic 44
    silent magic 36
audience participation, mind
    magic 44–50

B

Ballantine, Carl 20
Balloon Burst 138–9
Banana Split 108–9
Bangle and Ribbon 110–11
Bank Roller 128–9
Berglas, David 47, 48
Bertram, Charles 53
big magic 24–33
"bits of business" 17–18
Blackstone, Harry 31, 32
Blaine, David 15, 16, 36, 48
Bluff Book Test 70–1
Bobo, J.B. 189
Bow and Arrow 140–1
box jumpers 31
Boxes and Balls 80–3
Braue, Frederick 189
Brown, Derren 48, 59
Burton, Lance 24, 39, 59

C

Canasta, Chan 50
Card Prediction 130–1
Cardini 41
cards 8
    Card Prediction 130–1

card sleights 158–77
cheating at 15
Flying Cards 66–9
Jumping Card 174–5
Matching Cards 84–5
Name Spelling 176–7
Number Confusion 106–7
Tracker Card 171–3
Carlton 18
Carter the Great 31
Chain, Endless 150–3
changing one coin for another
186–7
cheating at cards 15
Chen, Juliana 42
children, as an audience 51
close-up magic 12–16
clubs, for magicians 15
cod magic 20
coins 8
    Coin Across 114–17
    Coin in Glass 94–5
    coin sleights 178–89
    Disappearing Coin 144–5
    Friendly Trick 86–8
    Slot-Machine Hand 119–21
comedy clubs 21
comedy magic 17–23
comedy mind reading 46
Compass, Magic 64–5
Conan Doyle, Sir Arthur 48
concealing a coin 178–81
controlling a card 165–7
Cooper, Tommy 19, 20
Copper Silver Coin Trick 188–9
Copperfield, David 20, 24, 31, 32,
    33, 55
Crayons, X-Ray 126–7
creativity 9
Culpitt, Fred 22
Cut and Restored String 74–6

D

Dai Vernon Book of Magic, The 14
dangerous magic 51–9
Daniels, Paul 20, 21, 31
Dante 31
Darnell, Nani 31
de Kolta, Buatier 41
Devant, David 12, 24, 26
Diminishing Cards, The 36
Disappearing Coin 144–5
Discoverie of Witchcraft, The
    (Scot) 57
Downs, T. Nelson 36
Dunninger, Joseph 50

E

Elmsley, Alex 14
Endless Chain 150–3
Erdnase, S.W. 15
Expert at the Card Table, The
    (Erdnase) 15

F

fakes 35
female magicians 42
finger palm, concealing a coin
    180
Fischbacher, Siegfried 24
FISM 39, 42
Floating Ruler 62–3
Flosso, Al 18
Flying Cards 66–9
Fogel, Maurice 48
force a card, how to 168–9
Friendly Trick 86–8
Frustrating Pencil 142–3
funny tricks 20

G

Gallup, Robert 59
Geller, Uri 48
gimmicks 35

glasses, tricks using
    Coin in Glass 94–5
    Glass through Table 146–9
    Levitating Tumbler 77
    Through the Glass 78–9
Goldin, Horace 22, 39
Great Lafayette, the 53
Green, Lennart 15

H
Harbin, Robert 26, 31
Hay, Henry 189
Henning, Doug 16, 31
Houdini, Harry 26, 32, 48, 53, 55, 57
Hoy, David 70
Huggard, Jean 189

I
illusions 24–33
It's Easier than You Think 35

J
Jarrett, Guy 26
Jarrett Magic and Stagecraft 26
Jarrow, Emil 22
Jay, Ricky 15
Jinx, The 50
Jumping Card 174–5
Jumping Toothpick 118

K
Kaps, Fred 16
Kellar, Harry 31, 55
King, Mac 21
Knife and Paper 102–3

L
Lavand, René 15
Le Roy, Servais 15, 42
Leipzig, Nate 16
Lenert, Tina 42
Levitating Tumbler 77
levitations 28
location

close-up magic 16
comedy magic 21
silent magic 39
Lonn, Johnny 20
Loop the Loop 92–3
Lyle, Cecil 31

M
magic advisors 35
Magic Castle, The (US) 15
Magic Circle, The (UK) 15, 26
magic clubs 15
Magic Compass 64–5
Magic of Robert Harbin, The 26
"Magic Ranch, The" 16
making a coin appear 184–5
making a coin disappear 182–3
Malini, Max 41
manipulation 34–41
Marvey, Peter 36
Maskelyne, J.N. 28
Matchbox, Rising 90–1
Matching Cards 84–5
McGee, Debbie 31
mediums 48
mentalists 44–50
Miller, Moi-Yo 31
mind magic 44–50
mirrors 24
misdirection 13
Moretti, Hans 59
Morritt, Charles 26
music for magic 36

N
Name Spelling 176–7
Napkin, Torn and Restored 98–100
New Modern Coin Magic, The (Bobo) 189
Nicola 31
Nixon, David 16
Not a Knot 124–5
Notable Number 122–3
Number Confusion 106–7

O
Overhand Shuffle 159–61

P
Paddling Knife 101
Paper, Knife and 102–3
Pencil, Frustrating 142–3
Pendragons, the 32
Penn and Teller 36, 59
Piddington, Sydney and Leslie 50
Pitchford, Richard Valentine 41
planning ahead 9
playing cards see cards
Pollock, Channing 39
Potassy, Paul 53
Practical Mental Effects (Annemann) 50
practice, importance of 12
    dangerous magic 51
    silent magic 35
    sleight of hand 157
preparation 8–9
Professor, The 14
props
    mind-reading tools 44
    for tricks 8–9
puns, using 17

Q
Queen of Coins, The 42
Quick Escape 96–7
Quick Release 112–13

R
radio, mind reading on 50
Randi, James 48
record-breaking illusions 32
restaurants, performing in 16
returning a card 164
Rising Matchbox 90–1
Robinson, William 55
ropes and string, tricks using
    Bow and Arrow 140–1
    Cut and Restored String 74–6
    Frustrating Pencil 142–3

Quick Escape 96–7
Quick Release 112–13
Solid Through Solid 132–3
Ross, Richard 36
Royal Road to Card Magic
    (Huggard & Braue) 189
ruler, floating 62–3

S
Salem, Marc 48
Salvano 36
Scot, Reginald 57
Secrets of My Magic (Devant) 26
Selbit, P. T. 55
selecting a card 162–3
shuffling cards 159–61
silent magic 34–41
situation comedy 17–18
sleight of hand 154–89
Slot-Machine Hand 119–21
Slydini 20
Solid through Solid 132–3
Soo, Chung Ling 55
Spina, Joanie 42
Spiritualism 48

stage presentation, illusions 24
Steinmeyer, Jim 26
stooges 22
Straw Cutting 134–7
string see ropes and string
stunts, mind-reading 48
swallowing tricks 53

T
Taking a Bow 104–5
Talma 42
Tamariz, Juan 15
television
    close-up magic on 16
    comedy magic and 21
theaters
    big magic in 31
    close-up magic in 16
    silent magic in 39
Through the Glass 78–9
Thumb Fun 72–3
thumb palm, concealing a coin
178–79
Thurston, Howard 31
Tibbles, Percy 55

Time Please 89
Toothpick, Jumping 118
Torn and Restored Napkin 98–100
Tracker Card 171–3
Tumbler, Levitating 77

U
"underground" magic 15

V
Vernon, Dai 14

W
Wessely, Otto 53
Williamson, David 15
Wilson, Mark 31
Wizard of the North 55
women magicians 42

X
X-Ray Crayons 126–7

Z
Zancigs, the 50
Zig-Zag Girl 31

Picture Credits

American Museum of Magic, Marshall, Michigan: pages 23, 40.
KJA Consulting, www.rainfall.com : pages 29, 37, 45.
Mary Evans Picture Library: pages 38, 52, 157.
Rex Features: pages 13 (Tony Kyriacou), 33 (Everett Collection),
49 (Robert Judges).
TopFoto, www.topfoto.co.uk : pages 19 (UPPA Ltd), 30, 54, 59 (UPPA Ltd).
Vinmag Archive Ltd: pages 56, 58.
All other photographs from the collection of the author.

The publisher apologizes for any unintentional error or omission in the
acknowledgments above and would be pleased to hear from any companies
or individuals who may have been accidentally overlooked.